"'History' is people who take steps to ensure that movements continue and find rails upon which to fulfill their vision. The history of SEND Canada is how key people enabled SEND International of Canada to begin, grow and have a large impact on the world through a small organization. Organizational charts and history make for dull reading but when you see the result of churches started overseas and many lives transformed by the grace of God then you realize that behind-the-scenes organization, recruitment, sound financial policies and careful screening really do make a difference. What is exciting about this book are the stories of the missionaries of SEND International of Canada."

Dr. Frank M. Severn,
General Director Emeritus of SEND International

"When one has known a mission organization virtually from its beginning, several of its past and current leaders, and many of its missionaries, it is an honour and delight to endorse this book. For anyone reading who is interested in knowing about the history of SEND International of Canada, Leander, a personal friend and acquaintance, has done an excellent job of detailing its background and birth. The answered prayers found here will encourage your prayer life."

Rev. Pete Peters,
Retired pastor and lifetime missions promoter

"As I am staying in the former SEND compound reflecting on the history of SEND International in general and SEND Canada in particular, I am reminded of the GI Gospel Hour during WWII, the formation of FEGC and eventually SEND. *Brought to a Place of Abundance* helps me to trace the footprints of God in the history of SEND. History is "His Story" written in the stories of so many people's lives. It is a living testimony of His faithfulness. Leander and Louise are witnesses to "His Story" in SEND Canada."

Dr. Peter and Mable Au,
Principal of Canadian Chinese School of Theology
at Tyndale Seminary

"Since its inception SEND Canada has faithfully provided the Canadian Church with a platform for global engagement. This book is a remarkable example of the truth, that while organizations do not create life, the best organizations nurture life through its people. *Brought to a Place of Abundance* traces the goodness of God down through the years and is a clear reminder that it is God's work through people that is an organization's greatest legacy."

Charles A. Cook, PhD,
Professor of Global Studies and Mission (Ambrose),
Executive Director of the Jaffray Centre for Global Initiatives,
SEND Canada Council Member

"This book speaks to the heart of real leadership and it comes from the heart of a real leader. Our brother, Leander Rempel, as a seasoned leader, has emulated the truths of this book in his years of ministry. You will find it to be a must read."

Dr. Roy W. Lawson,
Retired president of the Fellowship of
Evangelical Baptist Churches of Canada

BROUGHT TO A PLACE OF
Abundance

A BRIEF HISTORY OF SEND CANADA

LEANDER REMPEL
with Laverne Fehr

BROUGHT TO A PLACE OF ABUNDANCE
Copyright © 2014 SEND International of
Canada Inc.

Printed In Canada

ISBN: 978-1-4866-0476-0

Word Alive Press
131 Cordite Road, Winnipeg, MB R3W 1S1
www.wordalivepress.ca

MIX
Paper from
responsible sources
FSC® C016245

Cataloguing in Publication may be obtained through Library and Archives Canada

Dedication

I dedicate this book to my loving and lovely wife, Louise, a woman who accomplished the difficult task of raising three children while maintaining her intimate relationship with her Master. She is also one of the few women who can communicate Biblical truths to every age group. Truly a remarkable woman!

CONTENTS

SEND Commitment

SEND International's mission is to mobilize God's people and engage the unreached in order to establish reproducing churches.

To fulfill our basic purpose, we are committed to the following fundamental VALUES:

GOD-DEPENDENT:
We believe in the principle of our complete and prayerful dependence on God for the supply of our resources and enablement of our ministry. We are dependent on the ministry of the Holy Spirit as He uses the written and spoken Word of God. We hold the Bible to be the authoritative guide for faith and practice.

URGENT OBEDIENCE:
In light of the urgency of the hour and the lostness of people, we are committed to a life of obedience to God that calls us to serve Him, prepared to endure hardship, in order to proclaim the gospel and see His church established.

SERVANTHOOD:
As servants of our Lord Jesus Christ, we are committed to a life of giving ourselves for the sake of others including co-workers

and the community we serve, incarnating Christ's love by word and deed.

BELONGING:
We value each member of SEND and his/her work contribution.

INTEGRITY:
We strive to live morally above reproach, embracing honesty and fairness in all our relationships. We are committed to the highest standards of ethics throughout the organization and all aspects of ministry.

UNITY IN DIVERSITY:
We believe in the value of incorporating missionaries of many nationalities, backgrounds, etc. in the task of discipling the nations. We value a diverse membership of the Body working together in harmony towards the fulfillment of the Great Commission.

WORSHIP AND CELEBRATION:
We value God's grace and presence in our lives and ministry and express our gratitude through joyful, fervent and sincere praise, worship, and celebration of His providence.

(Taken from the SEND Canada Member Manual)

Acknowledgements

I would like to express my deepest appreciation to Rob "Mags" Magwood, who was the first person to encourage me to write this book. Every communication from the Canadian office, whether in person or via email that bore his name, repeated the request. He finally won. It has been a very pleasant experience.

Merla Gogel took on the tedious task of photocopying many of the SEND Board minutes and sending them to Homer, Alaska. Thank you, Merla.

A special thanks to Hannah Cox, who did an outstanding job of editing the manuscript while it was in draft stages.

Louise Rempel did a great job being my advisor.

The professional staff at Word Alive Press, especially Jen Jandavs-Hedlin, Amy Groening and Matthew Knight, has been a pleasure to work with.

I would be remiss if I didn't acknowledge the many fine missionaries serving with SEND Canada. It's because they are on the battleground that we as a home office exist. A special thanks to those who responded to our call for stories of success and challenges in ministry.

Last, but certainly not least, I want to thank Laverne Fehr. Without her, this book would not have been written.

Foreword

By Dr. Jean Barsness

Almost three hundred years ago, the first mission societies were birthed, with the stories of Count Nicolaus Ludwig von Zinzendorf founding the Moravian Mission Society and William Carey, the Father of Modern missions. Now, centuries later, it is estimated that worldwide 4,900 mission societies exist.

The stories of these early pioneers are indeed intriguing, and many, if not all the early mission societies, were launched within the context of unwavering surrender and incredible sacrifice. Far Eastern Gospel Crusade was no exception.

Ralph Waldo Emerson stated, "There is properly no history; only biography." Historian Ruth Tucker adds, "History . . . is a fascinating story of human struggles and emotions, intertwined with tragedy, adventure, romance, intrigue and sorrow." Tucker's words also describe the genesis of the Far Eastern Gospel Crusade

Within the context of the raging Second World War, GIs were serving in Japan and the Philippines. Their hearts were filled with passion for the Gospel and compassion for those whom their orders taught them to hate, but whom Jesus asked them to love.

FEGC began as the GI Gospel Hour in a morgue in the Philippines and on the 8th floor of a YMCA in Japan. Within a short time, GI Gospel Hour was changed to Far Eastern Gospel Crusade, and later to SEND International as we know it today.

Fifty years ago, SEND Canada began as an extension of SEND USA, with the first offices located in Toronto. SEND Canada's story is one of godly men and women of vision, leaders whom God had prepared and chosen. Among these, two names have become synonymous with the organization: Gordon Stimers, Chairman of the Board of Directors, and Leander Rempel, Canadian Director.

Leander's philosophies were basic and foundational: the Board of Directors is the gatekeeper. Mobilization is really discipleship. Mission societies are the arm of the church. Total dependence upon GOD for every decision. People without Christ are eternally lost.

As a member of the Board of Directors for the past thirty years, I have personally witnessed leaders whose lives were characterized by prayer and reliance on God.

On a personal note, I am grateful, more than grateful. I was diagnosed with cancer and Leander stopped everything to pray, asking God, for the sake of missions, to heal. He did.

I witnessed Gordon Stimers' dependence on God, evident at every board meeting. I clearly recall one specific Friday. It was the conclusion of the first day of board meetings. A decision was tabled because Gordon sensed we did not have the mind of Christ. Gordon urged us to get on our knees before the end of the day, to meditate on a specific Psalm, and to ask God for heavenly wisdom and discernment. We did as he asked. The following morning there was clarity on the issue and a unanimous decision was made without further discussion.

In giving us glimpses into the fifty years of SEND Canada, Leander has invited us to "come and see what God has done, his awesome deeds for mankind!…you brought us to a place of abundance" (Psalm 66: 5, 12b).

Half a century has come and gone. We report with humble gratitude that sixty-five percent of SEND International's leaders are Canadians. We are amazed with the goodness of God. Amazed that the country where the Gospel began in a morgue now has hundreds of churches, which today have become missionary senders.

In the midst of health issues, Leander Rempel has written, researched, and invited the reader to walk with him through the challenges faced in birthing and growing SEND Canada. It is the story of lives transformed, missionaries appointed, churches established and the power of the Almighty God evidenced.

May God powerfully use *Brought to a Place of Abundance* to inform, inspire, energize, instill urgency, and motivate readers to engage in the most important mandate and mission of all time: the declaration of the Gospel to the whole world.

Dr. Jean Barsness,
Missiologist, Professor of Global Studies
March 13, 2014

Part I

HISTORY OF GOD'S GOODNESS THROUGH
SEND CANADA 1963-2003

Introduction

*A*s World War II raged in the Pacific, there were American servicemen stationed in Japan and in the Philippines who saw beyond the war to the people living in these countries. They saw people whom God loved and for whom Christ had died. Their hearts were deeply and permanently touched with the love of God for these nations.

In order to meet this crying need, they formed the GI Gospel Hour. In the Philippines this became a weekly Saturday night evangelistic meeting held in a mortuary, one of the few buildings that wasn't gutted from the bombing. At the end of the day, the GIs would wheel the caskets out and set up the seating to preach the living Gospel to the physically living, but spiritually dead. After the meeting they would clear away the seating, wheel the caskets back in, and life or death would go on as usual.

Meanwhile, in Japan they rented the eighth floor of the Yokohama YMCA building, where precisely at 8 p.m. Saturday night the twin grand pianos would strike up the chords of "Jesus Saves," signaling that it was time to start the evangelistic meeting. The bars on the seventh and ninth floors emptied as the men attended their meeting. The burden for the lost in the Philippines and Japan lingered and grew after the war. The soldiers were compelled to action.

Far Eastern Gospel Crusade (FEGC) found its roots in this GI Gospel Hour, which is beautifully chronicled for us in the book *Through Open Doors: A History of SEND International (formerly FEGC)*, written by Mildred M. Morehouse.

While ministries were growing in Japan and the Philippines, FEGC also became established in Canada. This book is an attempt to capture the marvelous workings of our great God as he moved Canadians to become involved through prayer, finances and the act of personally giving their bodies as living sacrifices through the ministry of FEGC Canada, now known as SEND International of Canada (or simply SEND Canada).

1

The Foundation Of The Organization

*G*od places men and women in strategic places to accomplish His will in building His church. This can be seen as we look back at the beginnings of FEGC Canada. Three men from FEGC US preached in Bible institute chapels and classrooms, one of which was Grace Bible Institute (now Grace University) in Omaha, Nebraska. Some members of the student body were Canadians.

The three FEGC workers were Rev. Philip ("Phil" as he was known in the mission) Armstrong, Virgil Newbrander and Olan Hendrix, who all sacrificed time, energy, and (to a degree) family, as they preached their hearts out in public ministry. As a result, many young people seriously considered the Lord's will for them in mission service; the three workers effectively counselled these youth regarding their future.

Phil was the executive secretary of this fledgling mission organization. While he was still serving his country at the end of the Second World War in the Philippines, God placed a deep concern in his heart for the millions of people without Christ. He described how this concern became his passion through a life-changing incident. Phil, other servicemen, and Filipino guides were sent to look for bodies that had been sighted. Instead of "bodies," they came upon five living Japanese soldiers.

We rode in a truck to the Prisoner of War camp, with them huddled at our feet on the floor, naked and tied. I asked (or motioned) their ages. There were five of them. The two youngest were seventeen and eighteen.

I can't explain it—few people would understand. I'm not sure that you will, or that I do; *but I loved those men.* They were the people to whom we were sending missionaries five years ago. We loved them then.

But now we are taught to hate, *hate* them. […]

If only I could have shown them our glorious Lord! If only their darkened souls knew something of love—of God! I wanted as much as I have ever wanted anything in my life to get down with them and tell them of Jesus, the Prince of Peace, who died that they might live forever.

But I couldn't, and they, unless someone else tells them, will never know. It *hurts* to think how placid I have been when the *world* lies in darkness and despair because they have never known the joy of Jesus Christ living within them …

But their souls have as much right to freedom as ours.

I studied each face and in each my heart flared up with the words, "Christ died for thee … Christ died for thee … Christ died for thee … Christ died for thee … *Christ died for thee.*"

I felt as though I couldn't stand it.

I prayed until I had to look away in tears. Christ hadn't failed them. *We* had.

Now I've got to do something about it. I don't know what, but I am promising everything I have to our Lord to be used where He chooses. I'll never be satisfied with anything else now, even if it means burying myself in the heart of heathendom—literally as well as figuratively. Yes, I'll gladly go! I *have* to.[1]

How that played out on the North American scene is beautifully described by Dr. Walter Hansen in *Footprints*:

As a brash twenty-one year old, I walked into Philip Armstrong's office with my bride Darlene, hoping to gain his approval for our application to serve with Far Eastern Gospel Crusade (now SEND International) in the Philippines. It was spring 1968. The mission had a policy that a couple could not serve overseas unless they had been married for more than one year. Since we had only been married for six months, we were afraid we might not be accepted. Only the General Director could waive the restriction. Phil asked some very probing questions in his deep bass voice. Fortunately, he did approve of us. What I appreciate most about that initial encounter was Phil's promise that he would "keep an eye on us." For the next 12 years of my life, he never failed to live up to his promise.[2]

On one of his many visits to missionaries in the Philippines, Phil went with Walt and Darlene to their Bible studies. Walt writes,

Phil came to the university student center in downtown Manila to talk with some of our Bible study students. He did not spend much time in small talk. He went straight to the heart,

---

1   Givens, Elizabeth M. and Reapsome, James W., eds. 1984.*With my Heart There: Excerpts from the writings of Philip E. Armstrong.* Farmington, Michigan: SEND International.

2   Givens, Elizabeth, ed. 2007. *Footprints…Values of a man who walked with God.* Farmington, Michigan: SEND International, p.42.

not intrusively or abrasively, but with deeply felt and clearly expressed concern for the growth of the students he met. After he left, I followed his lead and moved more quickly and courageously to teach and lead the students.[3]

Walt did not return to the Philippines after the first term as Phil was urging; instead, he took the pastorate of a North American church. However, that did not deter Phil. He found other ways for Walter to participate in the mission, such as serving on the board.

Walter goes on to say,

After one of his visits [with Walter and Darlene in the pastorate], he wrote me a long letter filled with encouraging observations and piercing questions regarding my ministry. Unfortunately, I didn't keep his letter, but I remember the soul-searching I did after reading it. Why did I think I had to be at every meeting at the church? Why wasn't I delegating some of the ministry to gifted lay leaders? How would my family survive if I kept up this pace and didn't spend more time with them? Phil hit hard: iron on iron. And I love him all the more for his courage to speak truth into my life.

Through those years, Phil gave me books to read and to discuss with him.[4]

Walter was just one of the many lives that Phil touched through his passion to build the mission.

The second of the three men that God used to challenge the church to take action was Virgil Newbrander, who felt called

---

3   Ibid, p. 42.

4   Ibid, p. 44.

to go to Japan as a missionary. Both he and his wife, Jeanette, were deeply disappointed when they discovered that Virgil had Multiple Sclerosis. When he was approached by the mission to become the Home Office Candidate Secretary, he accepted the appointment with some reluctance; his heart was still in Japan. However, he gave it all he had. He kept a schedule that would put many men to shame.

The third man was Olan Hendrix, a powerful preacher with roots and connections in the business world. He felt mission organizations should measure up to business standards as far as efficiency was concerned. He introduced sound business principles and practices into the everyday operation of the mission home office, and eventually to the various fields of FEGC. Some missionaries felt this was unspiritual because FEGC was not a business. True, FEGC was not a business; it was and is an evangelical charitable mission organization that depends on God's provision for its funding. Still, to maintain its charitable status with the government it was necessary to have accurate practices. It was also important to have accurate records in order that supporting churches and individuals could see how their donated funds were used.

Olan also actively promoted the concept of all mission organizations in a local region moving into one building, with shared secretarial services and photocopying in the center of the complex. However, the mission community was not ready for this concept.

Phil, Virgil, and Olan powerfully communicated the need to bring the Gospel to the people of Japan and the Philippines as they toured Bible schools and churches. The students at Grace Bible Institute were deeply affected by the passion of these men and sought the Lord's will for their lives in response. Some of these students were from churches in the Evangelical

Mennonite Brethren conference (now called Fellowship of Evangelical Bible Churches). From ministering to students, it was an easy transition to ministering to the churches represented by these students. And so it was that the three FEGC workers rotated through churches in Langham, Dalmeny, Waldheim and Rhineland—all in Saskatchewan—and in Steinbach, Manitoba. Once the mission was accepted at the conference level, it had credibility in all of its churches. This was important when FEGC wanted to establish a mission in Canada.

The three men made it a priority that one of them would always be available to speak at missionary conferences and commissioning services in Saskatchewan and Manitoba. They did a tremendous job of representing the mission; however, their success took its toll on their personal lives and bodies as they went above the call of duty in their work. This resulted in incidents like one of the men falling asleep sitting upright in a chair while participating in family devotions in the home of one of FEGC's missionaries.

2

Early Years in Canada

God was strategically calling Canadian young people from Bible schools, churches, and business careers to serve with a mission that had not yet even started in Canada. Word was spreading at Bible institutes in Canada that a new mission had been started in the United States by former GIs. The Lord was calling Canadian young people to join the Far Eastern Gospel Crusade missionary forces in the Philippines and Japan. At this time, Canadian applicants filed their applications with the US office and were appointed by the US Council.

Before FEGC was organized in Canada, there were already Canadian missionaries who were serving in the Philippines and Japan. Ruth Miller from Ontario was the first Canadian FEGC missionary to arrive on the scene in Japan. Ruth married Conrad Miller and left for the field in 1950. Although her husband was not a member of FEGC, Ruth remained under FEGC's sponsorship in Japan.

Winnie Price from Ontario (of the Price & Jeans church planting team) was hard on their heels. Winnie left on December 1, 1951 aboard the ship, the "Sea Serpent," and arrived in Yokohama harbor eighteen days later. Winnie Price and Dottie Jeans (FEGC US) helped to establish five Japanese churches during their more than thirty-five years of service.

Dorothy Peters from Saskatchewan followed in 1952. She faithfully served in church planting in the Fuji Valley. This valley was steeped in Buddhism, with several large Buddhist sects headquartered there. The spiritual soil was hard, and there were many years of perseverance and seed-sowing. Growth was slow, but seeds did sprout, and Dorothy was privileged to see churches started along the valley. Dorothy recorded these stories from the Fuji Valley ministry:[5]

Mrs. Watanabe heard the gospel as a student but it wasn't till she was in her 80's when tracts were distributed door to door in her town that she decided to attend the monthly meetings conducted near her home. She became a seeker, believed, was baptized and became a member of the church and had meetings in her own home before she passed away.

Hideaki heard the gospel from his mother and older sisters. He realized he was not ready to die so felt afraid. When we had a meeting near his home he came and was saved, baptized, joined the church, went to Bible School and became a missionary.

Yuki watched an evangelistic movie and became a seeker, was saved, baptized and joined the church. She influenced her mother who also became a seeker and a believer but has put off baptism until her husband becomes a believer.

Mrs. Matsui hesitated because the whole family would misunderstand or even suffer shame.

---

5   Unless otherwise noted, this and all following firsthand accounts are based on personal interviews/email submissions in response to a call for personal stories, and/or missionary reports.

But not all of the activity was in Japan. Margaretha Reimer from Manitoba not only played a major role in the founding of Faith Academy in Manila, Philippines, but was also deeply involved in evangelism, discipleship and the establishment of the church there. She took her responsibility for the spiritual welfare of her house girls very seriously. Because of her passion and heart for evangelism, her house girls heard the Gospel and had the opportunity to trust in Christ as their Saviour.

Tom and Mary Tazumi from Manitoba and British Columbia were appointed as FEGC missionaries in 1959. They served in church planting and camp ministry in Japan until their retirement.

That same year, Janet Davis from Ontario was appointed for ministry in the Philippines. Janet's ministry was in the tribal region of Ifugao province, first at the Good News Clinic and Hospital as a nurse, and then in church planting. While missionaries from another organization were translating the Bible into the local dialect, Janet was instrumental in producing a hymnal of songs in that language, using their musical tonal scale.

As time went on, it became apparent that there was a need for FEGC to be incorporated in Canada. An organization had been receipting for FEGC missionaries but had indicated that this would no longer be possible. The Canadian government would not accept tax receipts issued by an American corporation, and the mission needed a Canadian address to demonstrate that it was truly a Canadian corporation. It was time to seriously move ahead with incorporation in Canada.

This began in Steinbach, Manitoba, where the pastor of the Evangelical Mennonite Brethren Church (now Cornerstone Bible Church), Rev. Sam Epp, and two businessmen in the church, Mr. George Loewen and Mr. Arnold Barkman, signed the Letters Patent. They formed the first board of Far Eastern Gospel

Crusade of Canada. The Canadian arm of the mission was officially established on November 12, 1963. Shortly thereafter, Rev. Epp and George Loewen resigned their positions on the board, enabling Phil Armstrong and Virgil Newbrander to become members of the Canadian board. When Arnold Barkman was no longer able to serve on the board due to illness, George Loewen was asked to take his place.

The first receipting as FEGC Canada was done in the office of Barkman Concrete (owned by Arnold Barkman). One of the secretaries there was charged with the task of issuing income tax receipts to those who had donated funds to the mission.

The Manitoba connection was fine for the formation of the mission in Canada, but did not facilitate its long-term growth. FEGC was founded as an interdenominational mission and needed a base broader than a single denomination from which to function. The minutes of the August 1966 board meeting state that "there was a brief discussion regarding the tentative plans for setting up a Canadian-Toronto Council, which would assist in setting up an annual banquet in Toronto for the Crusade, interviewing prospective missionary candidates and setting up itineraries for the candidates and missionaries." This set the stage for moving the board of directors from Manitoba to Ontario.

God knew about the need for a solid board, and He had already placed people in strategic places to serve Him as the need arose. God used the ministry of Olan Hendrix at the Canadian Keswick Bible Conference to rekindle a flame that had burned in Harold Fife's heart since an earlier time when he had committed himself to go wherever God wanted him to go. This resulted in two courses of immediate action: Harold began a relationship with FEGC, and he introduced Gordon Stimers, a Christian businessman in Toronto and member of his church, to it.

In the mid-'60s Harold resigned his pastorate to join FEGC as Minister-At-Large, a title he never liked and tried unsuccessfully to change—to him "at large" had no bearings.

Harold Fife's deep walk with God was reflected in outstanding preaching and teaching that challenged Christians to fulfill Romans 12:1—to lay their lives on the altar of sacrifice. He was greatly used by God in Canada, the United States, and all the countries where FEGC had ministries. He was a much-appreciated speaker at the Briercrest Fall Conference and church mission conferences, as well as a counsellor of on-field missionaries. His ministry extended to both missionaries and nationals.

Harold and his wife, Violet, were delightfully British. Violet accompanied Harold all over the world, and she always hand-carried a porcelain tea pot plus a china tea cup and saucer so Harold could have his afternoon tea precisely at 3:00. They stayed true to themselves and gained the respect and appreciation of those whom they served.

Harold Fife also arranged for Gordon Stimers to meet with Olan Hendrix, the FEGC US Director, who was eager to have FEGC better established in Canada. Gordon was asked to become involved in the establishment of FEGC Canada and now he was in a quandary. His home church, where he was heavily involved, did not favour his involvement in FEGC, yet he was being asked to help establish the mission in Canada. The church wasn't against missions—they were just concerned about losing their pastor, Harold, to the same mission. Gordon did what he had done through the years: he prayed and sought the Lord's direction.

Having asked God for guidance, he took the next step and visited the headquarters of the mission near Detroit. He was impressed by its orderliness. There were offices down each side of the building with the secretary's desk near the door of each office. After introductions, the secretaries returned to their desks; each administrative assistant knew their responsibilities. Their businesslike approach impressed Gordon.

During supper with the leadership, Gordon presented a case study in which a lady planning to serve with a certain organization met and developed a relationship with a doctor who was in the process of going with another mission. Gordon asked how they would respond to that situation. The answer was they would ensure that this was not a fly-by-night relationship, pray with her, then, if they were satisfied, assure her of their prayers for her and her doctor friend, sending her on with their blessing. Gordon became convinced that this was a mission that would work with others of like faith.

Gordon went to US board meetings for several years because he "didn't know how to run a mission." He found they had an atmosphere he enjoyed, which he hoped could be developed in Canada as well. This also gave him an opportunity to observe the functioning of the office.

Having thoroughly considered all the angles, he was now ready to commit himself. The first members of the Canadian Board of Directors (also called the Canadian Council) were chosen by Gordon. Arthur Clymer, involved in the wholesale food industry, was totally committed to missions and served on the board for a term of three years. William Crump was a teacher at Toronto Bible College. Ronald Miller, who worked for Ontario Hydro, served for a number of years as treasurer of FEGC Canada. Harold Fife was on the first board, as was Olan Hendrix. Gordon met George Loewen, a businessman from Steinbach, Manitoba, on the US Council, and seeing what a valuable contribution he could make, invited George to become a part of the Canadian Council. The other members were all from Ontario.

The whole process was something developed by God. Gordon spent much time in prayer. Because of his business situation, he was limited in the amount of time he could spend on developing FEGC Canada; he needed good men, and God provided, bringing FEGC Canada from vision to reality.

Gordon poured his heart and soul into the work and ministry of Far Eastern Gospel Crusade—so much so that he became known as "Mister Far Eastern Gospel Crusade of Canada." This godly man served as chairman of the board from August 1967 to November 2005, and then continued to serve as a board member. He gave more than 45 years of faithful service.

The Canadian office of the mission moved to a one room office in the basement of the Stimers' residence at 34 Jay Street, Toronto. For its own financial survival, the Canadian office needed to be totally dependent on the US office for public relations, receipting, recruiting, and processing of all personnel. This contribution was crucial to FEGC Canada and Canadian missions in general. However, it also negatively affected Canada's missionary community, because while the US office performed all these tasks for the Canadian office, the latter became an extension instead of a strong sending mission that used Canadian resources. The arrangement made a valuable contribution to the overall goals of the mission, but it didn't live up to the full potential of having a sending agency in Canada.

What was needed—a Canadian director—wasn't affordable unless FEGC could find one who already had personal financial support. It turned out that Russell and Betty Honeywell had the qualifications and finances to direct the mission organization in Canada.

.

3

Do Canadian Directors Grow on Trees?

*R*ussell Honeywell was in the US military in the Philippines when the GI Gospel Hour had its first meetings. He was one of the first missionaries to return to Manila to help set up Far East Bible Institute and Seminary (FEBIAS). His wife, Betty, and their three children joined once some housing had been set up. They served faithfully at FEBIAS, in church ministry and in administration.

The Canadian Council of FEGC invited Russell Honeywell to come to Canada for a three year term and in April 1975 Russell and Betty moved to Toronto. His responsibilities included oversight of the Canadian office, which was very small at this time, and, more importantly, making connections with donors and churches. Up to this point there had not been anyone in FEGC Canada able to give full attention to ministry in the Canadian churches and Bible school campuses. This was a real need if FEGC Canada was to become a well-established and viable entity standing shoulder to shoulder with the older mission agencies.

With their experience in FEGC and first-hand knowledge of the work of God in the Far East, Russell and Betty Honeywell proved to be God's choice to develop what had begun in Canada.

Before the end of their first term, the Canadian Council requested that Russell and Betty extend their service for another three year term. The Honeywells gave six years of service and saw FEGC Canada develop beyond having only a council and a part-time receipting secretary. It was now important to find someone who could build upon what had been started.

There is a constant tension between the home office of a mission and the missionaries on the field revolving around where you find the staff to man your home office. Missionaries don't grow on trees and this is doubly true of missionary executive staff. There is often an undertone of, "Which field are you going to 'steal' this one from?" The executive minutes of a meeting held on October 23, 1978 indicate that the Canadian Council was searching for a replacement for Dr. Russell Honeywell, who was planning to retire, and the tension ignited. At the February 18, 1980 meeting, the council appointed a committee to coordinate the search. Mr. Gordon Stimers approached Leander Rempel in late summer of 1980 to consider the possibility of becoming the next Canadian director.

Leander and Louise Rempel were serving in Alaska. Leander was the FEGC Area Director of Alaska and both he and his wife were deeply involved in ministry in the community. While their first reaction to the invitation from the Canadian Council was negative, they did feel that they needed to give it sincere consideration. After spending about a month in prayer, each came to the decision that God was asking them to serve in the Canadian home office. When they met with the Council in February 1981 in Toronto, they indicated their sense of God's leading to accept the call to be the Canadian director, but asked for a three year extension to finish the work in Alaska. There were just too many "irons in the fire" to leave immediately. The board agreed and gave them the extension.

However, the Canadian Council felt that the work in Canada was too important and the ground gained through the ministry of Dr. and Mrs. Honeywell too significant to just let it remain idle for three years. So, they started a search for an interim director. They were led by God to Rev. William Wallace, who was recently retired from being the head of the missions department at Ontario Bible College (now Tyndale University College & Seminary). As a result of this move, the work in Canada did not suffer in the interim. Wallace came to the job with a great wealth of wisdom, and knowledge, and had great influence in the Canadian mission scene.

Honeywell and Wallace both greatly contributed to the building of FEGC Canada and to the missionary cause. They made the most of the opportunities given them by school faculty to teach missions in the classroom. For years after Honeywell and Wallace left the ministry, Leander would meet people on campuses who would ask where they were and what they were doing. Whenever their names emerged in a conversation it always ended with a comment on the blessing and encouragement these two men had been to the students.

At the beginning of June 1983, Leander, Louise and two of their three children loaded a U-Haul truck and left Alaska bound for Ontario. They were the first people to rent a U-Haul to transport furniture out of Alaska.

At the same time, FEGC's International Council was struggling with the need to find a new name for the mission. The merger agreement between FEGC and Central Alaskan Mission stipulated that there would be a name change and neither of the original names would be included. After ten years of seeking, the International Council of 1981 finally decided on a name that subsequently was presented to the mission membership for approval. Far Eastern Gospel Crusade and Central Alaskan

Mission became SEND International on January 1, 1982. In a matter of months, a majority of the Canadian constituency of churches, schools, and fellow missions had accepted the name.

4

Board of Directors

*T*he board of directors is the gatekeeper of the mission. The board sets the tone for the organization. The CEO chosen by the board reflects who they are, since they will seek someone who has the same values and vision. This, in turn, will be reflected in the lives of those invited to become members. Hence, the values, vision and compassion of the mission begin with that of the board of directors.

Several years after the formation of the first council, the board made a deliberate attempt to invite people for membership on the board who were, *first* of all, deeply spiritual, and *secondly*, who were able to discern whether the applicant sitting before them had the potential of making a lasting contribution to the overall ministry of the mission. *Thirdly*, they chose men and women from various walks of life, including businessmen, pastors, college professors, accountants, and former missionaries. FEGC sought to choose people who were passionate about God's work, regardless of their financial resources.

God placed people on the board for a period of time, and then, for one reason or another, moved them on to other avenues of ministry. Through the gifts of the men who served on the board of directors, God expanded His work in Canada and overseas.

There were seasons when attendance at board meetings was low. Just before the Rempels arrived in Toronto, there were only three people who were regularly coming to meetings. There was an overall loss of impetus and commitment to seeing things happen. They had worked diligently and faithfully but were seeing limited results. Some were very busy in their primary ministry and were unable to give the necessary time to the FEGC/SEND Board of Directors. Some were on the board not out of commitment but because they were friends of a board member. This was simply the reality of the situation.

The Lord led several new members to the board from Ontario. Then a concerted effort was made to add some from Western Canada. Leander also wanted a woman on the council—until this time the board of directors was entirely male. Some objected to this move, feeling that the board should reflect the qualifications of an elder as outlined in I Timothy; since churches didn't have women on the elder board, neither should the mission. Leander reasoned that there were more female than male missionaries, so it only made sense that there would be a woman on the board. He also didn't see the board of directors as equivalent to eldership: the mission was not a church but rather an organization serving the church. Once a woman joined the board in 1983, it became apparent that this was one of the best moves they had made. Dr. Jean Barsness made a great contribution to the mission; her vast experience on the mission field, the trials God allowed in her life, her depth of spirituality, and her highly respected mentoring role in the Bible college scene amply prepared her to effectively serve on the board.

At the same time that Jean was invited to join, there was a need for a pastoral perspective on the board. This was provided by Richard Quiring, who was then pastoring a church in Regina, Saskatchewan.

Through the years God has brought businessmen and accountants to the board to provide expertise in their fields. Art Schmidt, Ted Cossitt, and Harold Barg have added tremendously to the financial operation of the mission.

John Klassen, an Ontario businessman, was an exemplary board member, doing his work well without any fanfare. He was a brilliant man who gave freely of his time and money. John was not only a strong influence on the Canadian board, but he also played a role in the international scope of the mission. It was a great loss when he was no longer able to serve as a board member for health reasons.

It was also a great loss when the Lord suddenly took Art Schmidt home. He was a turkey farmer from Saskatchewan who brought great spiritual depth to the board.

Faithful attendance at board meetings was a good indicator of commitment to the mission. It was also essential for board members to come prepared to be immersed in the mission's business. With busy lives, it took a deliberate effort on the part of each board member to leave their work and ministry behind for a few days and give focused attention to the ministry of FEGC.

It was not only "work, work, work and no play." The board met on Friday from 1:00 p.m. till 5:00 p.m. Then they would proceed to one of the better restaurants in Toronto (later London), paid for by one of the board members. Candidates were always invited, as well as the staff from time to time. Then the board would retire to various staff homes for a time of fellowship. Out of town board members were billeted in the various staff members' homes. Then they would reconvene on Saturday morning at 8:30 a.m. or 9:00 a.m. There was a genuine free spirit in the board meetings and with the staff; they genuinely liked each other's company. Quite often when the board members "came up for air" at coffee break or lunch, they were questioned by the staff as to what had been so funny.

Praise God for all the people that sacrificed time and money in Far Eastern Gospel Crusade of Canada.

5

The Fledgling Grows Up

*I*f the mission wanted to build a strong entity, it would have to transfer major responsibilities from the US office to the Canadian office. The process was just as difficult and fraught with danger as parents turning over responsibilities to their teenage sons or daughters, and the battle was the same. To the credit of the US office of FEGC, when Canada felt it was ready to assume responsibility for a specific task, the US office was prepared to give it up.

Leander felt it necessary that the office be developed to the point of being able to stand on its own two feet. He knew that the Canadian office would always be the "little brother," but he also knew that the little brother was capable of effective ministry to smaller schools, conferences, and churches in Canada. Limited personnel and finances naturally dictated that the US office, the big brother, give priority to that which, humanly speaking, would be most cost-effective.

Objections to having two home offices came mainly from those who weren't aware of the Canadian government's regulations and the untapped ministry opportunities in Canada's Bible colleges and churches. Knowing the Canadian scene, Leander and the board continued to move ahead in establishing a strong home office.

The first area tackled was finances. This involved the receipting process—which recorded contribution amounts, their proper disbursement, and the amount each donor had given year-to-date—so that reliable receipts could be issued for income tax purposes. When a missionary retired, the mission office had to confirm with the Canadian government the amount he or she had contributed to the Canada Pension Plan; this entailed keeping track of when a missionary went to the field for the first time, as well as all furloughs.

Computers are to finance what butter is to bread; one enhances the other. Jim Andrews had experience working with computers while at KRSA, a mission-owned radio station in Petersburg, Alaska. He used all his knowledge and experience, and then some, in assisting the development of a new accounting and receipting software program.

The transition of these different departments was fraught with danger. FEGC Canada didn't escape all of the trauma accompanying a venture of this kind. People in the US publicity department worked hard, but didn't always manage to include the Canadian addresses on the literature that was to be sent out from Canada. This meant that the Canadian constituency didn't always have ready access to Canadian contact information.

In addition, Canadian missionaries had to see themselves as equal partners in the overall missionary task, but they didn't always take this view.

Canadian missionaries took quite a while to see the Canadian office as a separate office, to understand that the mission now had two home offices. Those who had been processed through the US office had a harder time coming to this realization, but they eventually did.

At the beginning of the transition, the Canadian representative to the International Council would tap the conference table and say, "Let's think internationally." However, Canada hadn't yet made enough progress to take on major responsibilities. Even the staff didn't always remember that they were responsible for what happened in Canada; they would phone the US to make candidate decisions that should have been made in Canada. This was all part of the process of growing as a young home office and assuming more responsibility.

Another transition involved bringing the application process from the US office to Canada. This entailed all the work of answering potential missionaries' inquiries, sending out preliminary application forms, sending out reference forms, coaching potential missionaries in filling out the application forms and their doctrinal statement, and in general prepping candidates for their meetings with the board. At first, this was handled by Leander and Louise Rempel—until Eva Watt was added to the staff in 1985.

Eva approached SEND leadership about possible ministry opportunities upon completion of her studies at Tyndale Seminary. Leander spoke with the head of the Missions Department, who said of Eva, "If you're looking for a person to quietly accept anything you have in mind, you won't find it in Eva; she will not be a pushover."

Eva spoke her mind and made great contributions to the growth of the mission. When she was interviewed by the board—nine men and one woman, each proud of the fact that they were products of the Canadian church—in the middle sat one young Chinese woman. This was a most intimidating setting. Eva started her testimony by stating, "I'm a third generation Chinese Christian." You could have heard a pin drop. Eva was appointed by the Board to the SEND Canada office that day.

Eva Watt brought all her skillsets and spiritual depth to the Canadian office. She also brought a new culture to the office, which from the beginning integrated other cultures into the predominantly Caucasian mission. She opened a door to the Chinese community and impacted potential missionaries there, as well as in other cultures. She was able to bring growth to the Canadian office's application process.

The processing of applications was done by the staff to the point where they and the Personnel Committee felt they could make a recommendation to the board. The council wanted to maintain the responsibility of vetting applicants rather than giving that responsibility to a committee. This philosophy pervaded the board's mentality. They would ask deep questions of applicants when the latter met with them for an interview. They felt it was far better for someone to struggle with an answer while still in Canada than to have them discover on the field that it was not where they should be. At the heart of the council was a desire to really be sure that the applicants had been properly prepared to meet the challenges of a life of ministry in a foreign country.

The council minutes during those early years confirm this desire. There were times that the council made a conditional appointment if they saw that there was a gap in the preparation for overseas ministry. They would ask the applicant to take further training, do an internship in a church, develop their devotional life, develop a disciplined lifestyle, or perhaps wait on medical reports. There were times when the council put an application on hold. Sometimes a doctrinal position held by the candidate could lead him to work at cross purposes to the objectives of the field, and the council determined that the applicant would not be a fit for SEND. These were not always easy decisions to make, but the board was committed to making them prayerfully and carefully.

The due diligence given to the task before them was evidenced by the quality of the Canadians sent to the field. Dr. Sam

Rowen (SEND US) commented to Leander Rempel during a lull in the action at one International Council that "in three years' time Canadians [would] fill 65% of the leadership positions in the mission." Sam's prediction came true. This percentage grows in significance when you realize that Canadians made up only 13% of the total membership, as well as the complicated method SEND used to choose their leadership: when there was a vacant directorship on a field, the total field membership would be polled as to who they thought would make the best area director. There were various ways this polling took place. In the Philippines, all the members wrote the chosen name on a piece of paper. In some of the other fields, the field council divided up the entire body into a list for each council member to approach and seek the opinion of the missionaries as to who would make the best candidate for the job.

The council then approached either the top or the top two candidates for the job to see if he would be willing to serve in this capacity for a three year term. The mission felt that one year terms did not give the area director enough time to bring about changes that needed to be made, and that three year terms better suited their purposes.

Upon reaching a decision on a willing and qualified individual, the field council then approached the General Director to get his approval for the nomination. The name of the individual was placed on a ballot and the field voted to ratify the individual for the position.

It should be noted that this election process took place a year before the individual took office to allow time for him to exit his current position and prepare for his new responsibility. The thoroughness of the election process weeded out those not fit for the job, and time and time again, Canadians were singled out for leadership.

This is a very small sampling of the contribution of Canadian missionaries to the mission. There are many Canadian missionaries who have toiled patiently side by side with their international counterparts.

6

Relocation of the Office

The first FEGC/SEND Canada offices were set up in a room in a home or business. Since most of the office work was being done in the FEGC US office at the time, all that was needed was a place to do receipting and later some correspondence. However, in order for the organization to develop and take on more responsibility, a more permanent location was necessary.

Toronto was the natural location for the first rented office because most of the board members lived in the area. However, limited funds restricted the likelihood of finding suitable office space in the greater Toronto area. The office moved several times because of lack of space and increases in rent that surpassed the budget. Invariably, when the rental contract prevented an increase in the rent, the landlord would use updates in the common areas to add to the rental expenses. It became evident that serious consideration needed to be given to other location options.

All of these factors influenced the search for a new office location. The US office was located in Farmington, Michigan, in the greater Detroit area. Meetings with fellow workers in both offices meant at least a four hour drive. Would there be a suitable location to bring the two offices closer together? Along with the rental cost and space, housing for the office staff also needed to be brought into the picture. Would the staff be able to afford housing in the location chosen? Overseas missionaries are required to spend time in the home office before departure to their field of service and also while on home service. Office personnel would need access to an airport as they made trips to other parts of Canada and overseas. Which cities had easily accessible airport service?

A home office needed space to carry out the accounting, receipting and business functions of the organization. As missionaries would be added to the organization, there would be a need for space to train and provide pastoral care. A charitable organization is required by law to submit annual reports to the Canada Revenue Agency; these documents must be kept in office files. Space for filing these and other legal documents was needed.

Moving the office outside the greater Toronto area was a very touchy issue. The area director didn't want to referee the potential battle since the referee was sure to be injured in the process, so he asked the board to consider commissioning someone from outside of SEND to do a business evaluation of five potential areas in southern Ontario that would meet the criteria established by the board.

As the office staff and council members prayed and considered the need, the Lord led them to a gentleman by the name of Lloyd Reeb. Lloyd, a developer from Smith Falls, Ontario (near Ottawa), was of inestimable value to the council in the process of making the decision. He was unbiased as an outsider and could look at various options in southwestern and south central Ontario with mission objectives and needs in mind as he also trusted the Lord to lead in the whole process. He gained the deep respect and admiration of the SEND Council. In one of his reports, Lloyd said, "As a developer by trade, I always prefer to buy rather than rent—it's in my blood. However, in this case I wonder if we would be wise to negotiate the best possible long-term lease for a new office in London, Ontario" (October 1991).

In a memorandum to the Canadian missionaries on October 23, 1991, Leander Rempel wrote,

He [Lloyd Reeb] first did a study of nine or ten likely locations for the Canadian office; and then from the financial data gained, we reduced that number to approximately four cities. From there it was narrowed down to two, and then, ultimately, to one city. This whole venture has demanded a lot of research which was done in the office, that is Lloyd's office, and then numerous trips to the areas that we worked on. The final choice is *London, Ontario*.

Some of you good, loyal westerners will ask, "Did we consider any cities out west?" The answer to your question is, yes, we did consider moving the office west; however, there were some good reasons why we felt we should not move out of south central Ontario at this juncture.

Location decided—now where would the Lord have an office for SEND International of Canada? Just west of London on the outskirts of the town of Komoka, John Klassen discovered developers who were building a business complex. SEND was able to rent one of the units at a much more reasonable rate than they had paid in Toronto or even what would have been available in London. It was very accessible to the staff, who would be living either in London or in one of the many little towns within easy driving distance. The Lord so graciously meets the needs of His workers!

In August 1992, in a report to the Council, Leander Rempel thanked "John Klassen, who has done a tremendous amount of leg work and saved the mission a lot of money. It would have taken many more trips to the London area had John not been on location and ready to take care of numerous small items for us."

The Lord also provided furniture in a marvelous way. The furniture that had been used in Toronto was moved to the Komoka office, but with a larger space more was needed. A businessman in Manitoba provided the office with four large desks of pressed wood and shipped them via Penner International. This provision confirmed that the move had been the right choice, coming as the frosting on the cake.

The location proved to be just the right place for the office of SEND International of Canada! London had an airport which was ideal for domestic travel and it was a two hour drive to both the Toronto and Detroit international airports.

Day meetings were possible with the US office staff at either office or an intermediate meeting place. Before the days of Skype this was a great advantage over being in Toronto. The location was also accessible for missionaries coming to the office.

Housing costs and office rental enabled the staff and office to significantly lower their expenses. A commute in the Toronto area was at least an hour one way. Now, commuting time for the staff was greatly reduced.

The move to Komoka was made in August 1992. The offices were set up, and ministry moved forward until one disastrous day.

7

The Fire

The SEND Canada staff was adjusting well to their new office. They had plenty of space, a long-term lease, and adequate staff to cover most of the country. They were comfortably settled—perhaps too comfortable.

On May 13, 1993, local radio morning hosts were greeting their listeners with words that went something like this: "Hang on to your baseball caps. There is a stiff wind blowing out of the east with gusts estimated up to 95 kph."

Everyone was out of the office on mission business except for Bev Petriew. One of the tenants in the next office came rushing in and told her to get out because the whole building was on fire. Bev had the presence of mind to take the records and floppy disks and put them in the fireproof safe, and then got out of the building just in time. She stood at a distance, helplessly watching the whole building go up in flames.

Two men had been joining copper water pipes with a blowtorch in the wall at the unoccupied end of the building. They extinguished a small fire and assumed all was well, but by the time they returned from their lunch, flames had already spread to other parts of the building. When the flames reached the roof, a 40 kph wind blew the fire to the occupied end of the building. The building was already totally destroyed when the firefighters arrived.

All of the furnishings were destroyed in the fire. The fire was so hot that there was an indentation of up to an inch in the cement where each of the desks had been. The front of the refrigerator had melted in the intense flames. Anything below half a meter was untouched, but everything above was totally gone.

Amazingly, the boxes around the safe didn't burn and provided additional protection. The staff spent several anxious days waiting for the safe to cool down enough to open it. This object had been purchased for its fireproof quality; however, there is a big difference between sitting on a showroom floor and withstanding the heat of an intense flame. When the safe was opened, they determined quickly that the backup tapes were intact. The Lord had prompted Bev to act quickly, and His hand was evident as the staff began to reconstruct files.

Before the day was out, the landlord had already arranged for an office for SEND in downtown London, which cost him more than what SEND was paying in Komoka. Typewriters, a copier, and desks appeared, seemingly out of nowhere. The work continued on without stopping. Leander set the focus for the office: this was where they were going to be for now, and they would carry on.

At the board meeting shortly after the fire, Gordon Stimers opened the meeting by reading from Psalm 66:8 -15.

> *Praise our God, all peoples, let the sound of his praise be heard; he has preserved our lives and kept our feet from slipping. For you, God, tested us; you refined us like silver. You brought us into prison and laid burdens on our backs. You let people ride over our heads; we went through fire and water, but you brought us to a place of abundance.*
>
> *I will come to your temple with burnt offerings and fulfill my vows to you—vows my lips promised and my mouth*

*spoke when I was in trouble. I will sacrifice fat animals to you
and an offering of rams; I will offer bulls and goats.*

Gordon helped the board to think positively about the fire rather than negatively, and they exercised great faith in not being discouraged. Despite the circumstances, he exemplified the power of the Holy Spirit in the lives of believers and caused SEND to walk in victory rather than in discouragement.

Repeatedly the staff would go to Leander with stories of preserved documentation. Jim Andrews, the business manager at the time of the fire, was meticulous in filing and would always put records into the filing cabinet in a certain way. Unknown to him, the Lord had led him to file some upside down and backwards to ensure the needed figures were preserved. In recovering the account documents it was amazing to see how the Lord had arranged each page so that even though part of the document may have burned, the needed information was preserved on the unburned portion. Our God is amazing!

God had further surprises in store. Leander sent out a letter informing people of the fire. People responded with donations to replace the furniture and equipment. A business in Winnipeg provided a boardroom table for the refinished office.

In 1998 a double office became available in the same complex. The work was growing and there was a need for more space, so this was an opportune time to make a move. However, it would mean more furnishings were needed. One day, Jim was in a local Canada Trust. He came across a brochure indicating that the bankers were community-minded and liked to help people who were in need. While he was there, the bank was being renovated. The construction workers said they were going to throw away dividers. Jim asked one of the bank employees about the dividers and told them about SEND, a charity. The bank employee asked Jim to complete a form requesting used office furnishings and said it would be considered.

In time the application was approved. Jim and Leander thought they might go pick up a few partitions and a desk, but they still rented a big U-Haul and drove to a warehouse in south London. They pulled up to the building. They were shown a big warehouse filled with desks and other office furniture. They wondered what was available for them to take—maybe just a few of the desks that sat over in one corner. When they asked the warehouse supervisor what was available for them to take, to their utter surprise, he told them to take anything they wanted! Now was the time to dream dreams! There were glass corners and room dividers. There was a fireproof two-drawer file cabinet. There were metal desks. Just amazing! By nightfall, the U-Haul was full! This was God's warehouse and He was blessing SEND Canada.

When they brought the furnishings to the office, they were asked how much all of this cost. Just the price of gas and the U-Haul rental! The SEND office is still using some of this furniture after many years.

The furnishings in the office had come a long way from the sparseness of the first Toronto office. The inventory of that first office consisted of a French/English typewriter, two desks with chairs, one office divider, a mimeograph machine, and a Thermo fax that only occasionally worked. That was it. The Lord had provided in an abundant, unexpected way at just the right time. What a wonderful provision from the Lord!

There are some things in life that God's children will never understand. In such situations, He reminds them of His sovereignty so that they can rest in Him.

Betty and Russell Honeywell

Ione Essery in a Toronto office – always a cheery smile and greeting for anyone coming through the door

Eva Watt served ably in the Personnel Department

The fire in May 1993 totally destroyed the SEND office

The fireproof safe after the fire

Board of Directors, November 1993. Standing l – r: Richard Quiring,
Art Schmidt, Jean Barsness, Terry Tiessen, John Klassen,
Leander Rempel, Claude Pratt, and Gordon Stimers.
Seated: Frank Severn, General Director

*Gordon Stimers and Frank Severn at the November 1993
dedication of the new office facility after the fire*

*Louise Rempel served as Candidate Secretary as
well as frequently hosting guests in their home*

John Klassen was recognized for his faithful service with SEND

*One of the many short-term teams that
served with SEND missionaries*

The staff met on a regular basis for ministry updates and prayer

From time to time, the staff enjoyed fun times like celebrating a birthday

1998 dedication of SEND Canada's current double office

Jean Barsness, Board Member, honouring Leander and Louise at
the Induction of the new Canadian Director in 2004

Leander hands over the directorship to Mags

Leander and Louise Rempel at their 2004 retirement

An assortment of SEND Canada logos from over the years

Part II

Blessings and Learning Along the Way

"People are our #1 resource."
- Leander Rempel

8

The Purpose of the Home Office

*H*ow would an office function without the valuable ministry of secretaries and administrative assistants? It is essential to have accurate accounting of funds, and donors need to be notified that their donations have been received. SEND has been blessed to have secretaries and assistants who have been used wonderfully by their Lord.

Mrs. Gwen Reed and Mrs. Dora Russell served as secretaries while the office was still in Toronto homes. Mrs. Norma Dorey was already connected with FEGC through her husband, Gordon Dorey, who served on the Board of Directors. She became more involved through ministry in the office. By this time, the office had moved into rented facilities in Toronto.

Ione Essery was a delightful person to have on staff. Ione came to SEND in 1980 from another religious organization, and with her came years of training, office skills, and experience. This added greatly to the overall ministry of the office. Her bright and bubbly demeanour went a long way toward making callers feel that they were important. Ione retired in 1988, but continued to keep in touch with SEND missionaries and pray for them. Her letters have brought joy to many missionaries.

As the ministry grew, so did the need for additional home staff. Cathie Miles (née Ten Brinke) had been serving in the

Philippines but needed to remain in Canada because of medical reasons. Her overseas experience prepared her to lead summer student teams, and she was also effective in recruiting new missionaries.

The administrative staff in Toronto also included Robert Ang, who served as business manager, and Duane Barsness, who was a valuable asset in recruiting.

Beverly Geldart (née Petriew) joined the Canadian office staff in 1989 to serve as executive secretary to the Canadian director. However, her skills enabled her to serve in various other capacities during her ministry with SEND. Bev and Andrew Geldart served together in campus ministry and in leading several short-term teams. It was out of these short-term ministries that they gained a passion to personally serve overseas.

Esther Rowe volunteered for 2 ½ years as Leander's secretary when the office moved to the London area.

Merla Gogel transferred from Japan, where she was involved in church planting, to the home office, where she worked as the administrative assistant to the director.

Jack and Ella Sailor did a great job of establishing a church in Dawson City, including the building of a church structure. When they came home, they joined the personnel department. Andrew Geldart was used by the Lord to recruit missionaries and lead short-term teams to various parts of the world where SEND ministered. Rod and Eileen Seib started ministry in Taiwan; when family needs required that they return to Canada, Rod served as manager of member care for a number of years in the home office. Jake and Lillian Leyenaar came from a successful ministry in the Philippines and then served in the home office in finance and personnel, respectively. Heather Ficzere (née Quiring) worked in the finance department until her marriage. Audrey Lawrence has laboured faithfully in finance and donor relations.

Member care is a very broad subject. It includes placing people in the right assignment; making sure that the person feels loved, respected, and valued; and providing empathy and support as the person faces inevitable challenges. This takes forms that look as different as the members themselves. The office staff needs to be sensitive to each missionary's needs and know how best to come alongside them. Many have benefited from the care extended to them and have come through difficult situations as better servants because of it.

The mission organization and its home staff exist for the purpose of reaching the nations with the Gospel. Their work in the home office makes it possible to send out new missionaries and to enable those missionaries to continue in overseas ministry.

9

Recruiting

*A*number of years ago a Bible college in Canada decided that they would do missions a big favour and hold a recruiting seminar. They invited missions to send their best recruiters to the seminar. The mission leaders responded with great delight. When the appointed day arrived, the Bible college president and the main speaker mounted the platform and turned to the audience. After they were seated, the college president leaned over to the main speaker and said, "If these are our best recruiters we are in deep, deep trouble." He was referring to the preponderance of tired gray-haired missionaries that the missions were recycling, and the total lack of vibrant young people. Too often mission organizations have older missionaries in recruitment while younger missionaries are serving on the field.

It is intimidating to go onto a college campus for the purpose of recruiting. The students are all frightfully busy and they just get busier when they spy yet another mission arriving on campus. It almost becomes a game played by the missionaries and the students: the students see how long they can go without talking to a missionary. It is estimated that 90% of the students on a Bible college campus will never talk to a missionary. Students have commented that they hear and see many missionaries on campus and that each organization wants to recruit them; eventually, the easiest thing to do is avoid contact as much as possible.

SEND leadership grappled with the dynamics of the recruitment situation: the field was calling for more workers, young men and women were inundated with needs from around the world, and the recruiters or mobilizers were caught in the middle.

SEND Canada's philosophy on recruiting focused on ministry rather than on signing up new potential missionaries. The ministry was to the whole student body, regardless of whether they were interested in missions or in SEND or in another mission organization. God chooses ordinary people to do great things for Him. SEND representatives did not narrow ministry to the top ten students in the school. They were expected to have a genuine interest in each individual and their walk with the Lord. Ken Guenther's experience reflects this:

> God used Leander to lead me to SEND. He invited me for a Coke in the lounge at Briercrest in my 4th year there and made it clear that SEND was interested in me. I had been a transfer student from PRBI, and had never heard of SEND until I transferred to Briercrest. At my graduation from Briercrest in spring, there was Leander again together with someone from the International Office and everything they told me about SEND matched the type of mission agency I was looking for.

SEND representatives were not allowed to stand or sit behind a counter or table, nor were they allowed to read a book while at the display. Their total focus had to be on the students they were meeting. They needed to purpose to serve a student, rather than determining whether a student could serve the mission's purpose.

James Leschied says

[My] first introduction to SEND International was at Nipawin Bible Institute sometime between 1989 and 1992. The SEND representative spoke in the chapel service and agreed to an interview that I needed to do for a class assignment. Each year the representative would come through and our acquaintance grew as well as my respect for him. In 1993 at a mission conference at Briercrest Bible College, God was speaking to me about missionary service. The same SEND representative was there and that is where my future relationship with SEND began.

Short-term programs were seen as a form of recruiting. They have been criticized as being wasteful of human talents and finances; however, an effective short-term program challenges people to serve on the mission field by providing as much exposure to ordinary missionary life as possible. An analysis of the list of all SEND career missionaries indicates that 48% have had previous short term experience or have transferred from another ministry.

A summer program could be designed for those who might never return as a career missionary. One short-term worker who was destined to take over his father's car dealership had a terrific summer in Japan. He learned about missions in a difficult mission field and he will never be the same.

Clive and Sharlane Donaldson were asked to consider returning to Alaska for ministry after serving as summer workers.

[The invitation] gnawed away at Clive over the following winter, while he pursued opportunities to teach Bible and not work in administration, in many places in the world but NOT Alaska. This was the Donaldsons' second year at Prairie Bible Institute (PBI) in Three Hills, AB. The SMP (Summer Mission Program) experience had been good and they had come to understand first hand that God was using ordinary people in missions, and that not all these folks were gifted evangelists or preachers. Having gone to Bible college with no intention of spending their lives in mission service, this was already a big step. But administration in Alaska just didn't seem to be the right direction.

In the end, the Lord did direct them back to Alaska, where they have served faithfully for many years.

SEND found that recruiting was best done as a team, combining older missionaries and young people. The older missionaries had served overseas and were now living in Canada or were on home service; they brought a wealth of cross-cultural experience. The young people had just made a decision to serve overseas, had just returned from a short term stint, or had just completed their first term. They complemented each other.

Recruiters will generally recruit the kind of people they are. Therefore, it was important for SEND Canada to diversify who was sent onto the campuses. God had gifted some of His children for this ministry and He brought them into SEND at just the right time.

The recruiting team was intentional in the development of Bible college chapel presentations. These presentations were creatively presented in the form of skits and drama to address current issues that were in the minds of students. Some of these topics included "Is finding God's will like nailing Jello to a tree?" and "Is God fair for sending people to Hell?"

Prayer was essential from start to finish. Jesus said, *"Ask the Lord of the harvest, therefore, to send out workers into his harvest field"* (Matthew 9:38). The team met for prayer the week before departing on a campus ministry trip, and then spent time in prayer during the trip.

During the period of time from 1972 to 1982, the number of missionaries in Alaska went from around 30 to 104. Neither the Alaskan director nor the home office recruited all those missionaries; the Alaskan missionaries did. The Alaskan missionaries were so enthusiastic about their work that it was contagious. They simply operated on the basis that people come first—not the organization. While these were not members of the SEND Canada recruiting team, it does show that home service missionaries on a recruiting team can be a tremendous asset. SEND Canada tried as much as possible to include home service missionaries on their recruiting teams.

Some people said it was awfully expensive to send a team rather than only one person to recruit. The command of Christ to go into all the world with the Gospel has always involved a cost, including a monetary one. This didn't mean reckless spending of money, but money was needed to challenge God's people to become involved in His work and to prayerfully consider cross-cultural ministry.

Having a philosophy of recruiting didn't mean instant results. It took time—often years—to build relationships with potential missionaries. SEND had a good, growing system. Did SEND get more recruits than other organizations? That isn't known. However, the SEND goal was and is to minister to those with whom they had contact. These years were an opportunity to build into the life of the person; a time to encourage them in their walk with the Lord, in their ministry in the local church, and in the development of their gifts and skills. Virgil Newbrander aptly stated, "Secular organizations use people to build great organizations; but the Christian mission should use the organization to build great people."

Church/Mission Relationships

*I*n the early development of SEND USA, advisors forced the mission to consider where they fit into God's global program of evangelism. Over what part of that program would God want SEND to assume responsibility? They felt that taking on the whole world would spread them too thin. SEND USA zeroed in on the church. When SEND Canada came on the scene it was natural to follow that precedent.

The commitment to the church resulted in slogans like this: "Where the church already exists we will assist it, where it doesn't exist we will start it." SEND Canada, along with its American co-workers, didn't concern itself with the success others were experiencing with radio, Biblical education, or feeding hungry children; these were all right and good and deserved the support of the Christian public. But they were not where SEND felt God was directing them to focus their ministry.

This commitment to establish the church resulted in the start-up of ABCCOP (Alliance of Bible Christian Communities of the Philippines).

Far Eastern Gospel Crusade (FEGC), now SEND International, started church planting missions in the Philippines after WWII, birthing several churches in the Quezon Province,

Marinduque Islands, and Cagayan Valley. OMF started thereafter; primarily in the Batangas province, Bicol province, and the Mindoro islands.

Sensing the need for fellowship among these churches, both OMF and SEND decided to form an association whose primary purposes are fellowship in the ministry and continuance of the mission.

In November 1972, the group was formally registered with the Securities and Exchange Commission of the Philippines as the Association of Bible Churches of the Philippines (ABCOP).

Through the years, the organization felt a need for a stronger community. Along with major amendments in the by-laws, the name was then changed to Alliance of Bible Christian Communities of the Philippines (ABCCOP) in 1989.[6]

Meanwhile in Japan, missionaries were also involved in establishing churches. This eventually led to the formation of NIHON SHINYAKU KYODAN (NSK), the association of indigenous churches developed from their ministry.[7] Missionaries worked with Japanese pastors in reaching out to other areas that had no Gospel witness. Over time, several cooperative associations merged into a single association, the Japan Evangelical Missionary Association (JEMA).[8]

---

6   Alliance of Bible Christian Communities of the Philippines, "History." Accessed April 3, 2014, at http://www.abccop.org/history.html.

7   "Records of SEND International – Collection 406." Accessed April 3, 2014, at http://www2.wheaton.edu/bgc/archives/GUIDES/406.htm.

8   "History of the Japan Evangelical Missionary Association." Accessed April 3, 2014, at http://www.jema.org/joomla15/index.php/who-we-are-topmenu-27/15-history-of-the-japan-evangelical-missionary-association.

SEND Canada was vitally involved in the overall focus on church ministry. There were Canadians who took on leadership in going into these places of new ministry. John and Sharon Wicker were at the forefront in going into Krasnoyarsk, Siberia and then to Ulan-Ude. James and Molly Leschied were also a part of the initial thrust into Krasnoyarsk. Ken and Bertha Guenther began service in the Philippines and then transferred to Far East Russia (FER) at the request of SEND International leadership. The work in FER had progressed to the point where they needed an area director when Dwayne King (SEND US) was transferred to the International Office.

John and Sharon Wicker served in Russia.

We do see that God used us in what we've now come to see as the pioneering days of SEND's work in Russia. God chose us to be the first SEND workers into central Siberia to help in establishing the Krasnoyarsk Bible Institute. Did we do that single-handedly? By no means! But God did place us there as the first ones and the ones to lead the team from the beginning. He allowed us to work alongside two local graduates of that Bible school in the nearby city of Divnogorsk, and we saw that church grow from a few believers in a crowded living room to 100+ in a beautiful church building overlooking the Yenisey River valley. Later, God used our willingness to go into new places to help open up SEND's work in Buryatia.

John was able to get close enough to the two pastors in the Divnogorsk church to have a sharp disagreement which ended in a prayer meeting. From that prayer meeting, they saw God answer many prayers for growth in the church. Sharon saw God use her weakness and the need for a ladies' Bible study group to start with women taking turns to lead other women in studying God's word—something the Russian ladies had never done before, and something that knit all of their hearts together for all time and eternity.

SEND International committed to work with the Russian Baptist church when many other agencies were reluctant to collaborate with this national church. By God's grace, this working relationship has brought rich blessing to both SEND and the church in Russia!

SEND Canada promoted the work in Russia, especially Ukraine and Far East Russia, by sending teams of laymen and pastors to observe and become involved financially. They experienced firsthand the challenges of the ministry and of day to day life in a cross-cultural setting. The team members realized what the missionaries had to cope with in the midst of the work in FER, and understood the need to uphold these workers in prayer. As far as the Canadian home church was concerned, the return of the pastor and laymen with their positive reports considerably raised the church's interest level in, and their support of, the overseas ministry.

As the team was exposed to the ministry of the church in FER, they became burdened for the church there and later became involved financially and prayerfully. The exposure also raised the team's commitment to the missionaries whereby they were ready to encourage in any way possible the latter's ongoing efforts.

SEND Canada led a number of vision trips to Russia and Ukraine. These trips were taken by pastors and Christian businessmen. They served two purposes: one was to get the pastors and businessmen excited about the ministry overseas, and the second was to encourage the missionaries to carry on. Interaction with vision teams gave the missionaries a sense of partnership with the churches in Canada. It also heightened the interest of the Canadian churches in becoming involved prayerfully and financially.

Some people consider there to be no difference between the church and SEND International, but SEND members do not fall into this category. There is a strong commitment on the part of SEND Canada to the local church. The church is the one commissioned to go into the whole world and they are responsible to send out their missionaries; SEND is an arm of the church and assists in this ministry, but it is not the church itself. SEND makes much of missionary services in the church and requires its missionaries to maintain contact with the church through personal interaction, letters, and other media communication. SEND felt that there was progress in promoting these relationships but knew there was always room for improvement.

As an example of SEND's commitment to the church, they often found that Bible college students would apply to the mission without first talking to their local church. SEND would insist that they talk with their local leadership before continuing with the application, which churches appreciated.

SEND also has sought to develop a relationship with churches through its public ministry. Most of this ministry was left on the shoulders of the Canadian director. He would combine ministry at church missionary conferences with recruiting on college campuses as much as possible. This enabled the churches to get to know SEND and vice versa.

//

Finances and Fundraising

his is a difficult subject to introduce. Finance is typically a touchy area of life. However, it is unavoidable and it must be included in the narrative of FEGC/SEND's development.

SEND Canada has seen some great successes and miserable failures on the part of the administration. On the one hand, receipts went from $513,844 in 1983 to $2.6 million in 2003. Part of this was reflected in the increased number of new missionaries who raised funds to serve overseas, and part of it was the concerted effort of the Canadian director to raise funds for projects.

On the other hand, there was the financial picture in Canada itself. That was an exercise in frustration because support for the home office is not a priority for most Christians. SEND Canada personnel tried every which way to get the Canadian Christian public excited about the home office. At one time they calculated the overhead cost of the office in terms of cost per square foot and then asked people to commit to support a certain number of square feet on a regular basis.

Another factor contributing to the frustration was the absence of a setup fund; most businesses, when they start a satellite office, fund it and expect that the satellite office is going to go into the hole. FEGC never did that; the absence of a start-up fund was a big obstacle for this fledgling mission to overcome.

FEGC Canada was responsible for raising its own funds from the beginning. Consequently, it faced many International Councils apologetically because Canada was in the hole financially. Added to this was the strong SEND International principle prohibiting deficit spending. In the light of all the ramifications, the SEND Canada Council prayerfully permitted deficit spending, knowing that some expenditures were necessary in order to establish the office.

This was an encumbrance for many years. The SEND Canada leadership in the board of directors and in the executive staff persevered and continued to trust the Lord to provide not only for the deficit but for the advancement of the ministry of SEND Canada. They sought to cut expenses wherever possible and to make the need of office funding known to churches. The Lord honoured their perseverance and faith and their commitment to integrity and transparency. He provided over a period of years, to the point where the deficit was eliminated.

In Leander's Canadian Director's Report to the International Council in November 1999 he said,

> For years I came to this forum and reported that our General Fund was still in a deficit position. I was dutifully reminded, and correctly so, by the International Treasurer that SEND policies did not permit deficit spending. At last I can say we are no longer in a deficit position—*all glory to God!* I always maintained, and still do, that the reason for the deficit was spiritual and not physical. I am not trying to duck responsibility, and never have, nor am I saying that we are more spiritual now than then. What I meant was that God could easily change the negative balance into a positive one and that prayer was a key to that. God has used at least four human factors to turn the picture around:

4.1   A treasurer who watches our spending.

4.2   We praise God for finally settling our claim for damages due to the fire on May 13, 1993.

4.3   God blessing us with very high staff support. In addition to God's blessing I would like to commend our staff who have worked hard in securing it .…

4.4   Increased mission income.

Finances are always a touchy subject and it is especially true that Christians and missionaries vary greatly in their philosophies on handling funds. This difference of opinions prompted someone to say that one of the beauties of heaven is that he would stand upon the gold and it would not be the pressure that finances brought to bear on Christian ministries.

SEND Canada received advice from many different quarters on how to solve their financial problems but they had to walk this path alone with the Lord as He led and taught lessons during the process.

Through the years SEND Canada has seen God provide for the ministry of many missionaries, for many projects, and for the needs of the operation of the home office. He has taught His people to depend upon Him in each situation. This is reflected in one of the values of SEND International which partially states, "We believe in the principle of our complete dependence on God for the supply of our resources and enablement of our ministry."

/2

Prayer

*I*f you were to read the Council minutes, you wouldn't have to read very far before a theme would surface. From the first meetings to the present, prayer has very much been a part of the development of FEGC/SEND in Canada.

As chairman of the board, Gordon Stimers would make a list of the board members present at the meeting; by the end of each one, every member had prayed twice. Not only did they pray for the business at hand, but Gordon made sure that the missionaries were included in the prayers of the board members.

The whole meeting was bathed in prayer. This set the tone: it changed the attitudes of the members on the board, it moved them away from business mode, and it also impacted their lives. Impressed by the emphasis on prayer, one board member started to lead meetings in the same way. When another board member began ministry at a Bible college, he also followed the example set by Gordon. Another said, "You know, when I came into this mission I was sort of a nominal Christian; this has changed my life."

When the council faced tough decisions during the meeting, Gordon would stop the meeting to pray for the solution to the problem. Jean Barsness was very impressed with the way all matters were laid before the Lord.

The board members also desired to have the church pray for missions. Through the years there have been efforts to establish prayer groups across Canada to pray for SEND missionaries and the ministry. This eventually developed into a monthly prayer bulletin, *Push Back the Darkness*, which is mailed or emailed to anyone interested in joining the prayer ministry.

In the same Canadian Director's report in November 1999 Leander shared

> When we last met I reported that we had approximately 60 people enrolled in the prayer initiative called *Push Back the Darkness*. In the three intervening years this has grown to over 100 people. Not only have we grown in numbers, but the quality and commitment of this group continues to grow. The overall number includes individuals and small groups. Of significance is the fact that the number of groups continues to grow.

All missionaries were required to have thirty prayer partners before they could depart for their field of service. This was just as important as raising funds for their ministry. The missionaries were asked to pray for the partners just as they invited prayer from them. They were going into the frontlines of spiritual battle and needed the prayer support of those in their home country.

Not only were missionaries required to promote prayer, but the home office staff met daily for prayer during the noon hour. All aspects of the mission were brought to the Lord. Prayer items mentioned usually contained everything from mission leadership on the field to the needs of the missionary, whether on the field or on home service. There were times when the office staff became aware of a sudden emergency situation, and a special time of prayer was called.

Quoting once again from his report, Leander shared

Another plus in the overall prayer emphasis is that the quality and intensity of staff prayer times continues to grow. I remember well the times that our praying was legislated, stiff and formal. We would each take one missionary card from the box and dutifully pray for our missionary. I'm happy to report that our praying is much more spontaneous and exciting. We had a day of prayer some weeks ago and during that time our recruiting teams knelt as we stood around them and committed their times on the campus to the Lord. I believe there is a growing significance to our praying.

This emphasis on prayer started with the top leadership of SEND. Phil Armstrong deliberately sought out people to pray fervently for the mission, the missionaries, and the people of the nations. He found individuals like a lady in Manitoba who, after doing the dishes, folded up her apron, and then asked Mr. Armstrong to tell her about "her" nations for whom she prayed regularly. She and a widows' group in Steinbach, Manitoba spent hours in prayer for missionaries and the lost, unreached people of this world. Her reputation of getting answers to prayer was such that when her grandson was approached by an interschool Christian fellowship leader to ask his grandmother to pray for snow for a retreat, he asked how many inches they wanted. There were many others like this dear lady and her widow friends who fervently prayed for the nations in which FEGC/SEND missionaries were assigned.

One area director said that when Phil Armstrong came to the field, he insisted on praying through the entire field, person by person, so that the entire missionary force was covered by prayer.

13

The Call to Cross-Cultural Ministry

*T*he leading and confirmation of the Lord in the lives of men and women for overseas ministry is crucial to their perseverance in the spiritual battle. God leads people individually and uniquely.

Terry and Gail Tiessen share how God led in their lives.

Gail and I were both studying at London College of Bible and Missions (LCBM) with a view to serving as missionaries. During our student days, while we were dating, Virgil Newbrander visited the school a few times and we enjoyed learning from him about the work of FEGC. I had thought I would go back to India to serve, as my parents had done, but was uncertain about the kind of missionary ministry God had designed me for. In my final year, a missionary teaching in a seminary in Latin America came to campus and spoke of his work. I felt a strong attraction toward the sort of ministry he described. Gail and I then began to contact missions which seemed a good fit, and to inquire about their opportunities for this sort of ministry. Virgil told us about the work at FEBIAS (Far East Bible Institute and Seminary) in Manila and we grew steadily more interested both in FEGC as a mission, and FEBIAS as a ministry.

After we had graduated from Bible college and both gotten university degrees, I did an MA at Wheaton, keeping in contact with Virgil throughout that time. After Wheaton, I was invited back to teach at LCBM for a year while a faculty member was on sabbatical. FEGC encouraged me to get that experience even though it would delay our departure. During that year, we coordinated a visit to the FEGC office in Farmington for a number of the students at LCBM. We were very pleased with the spirit we met among the staff there, and with how well they presented the mission to the students who were with us.

Missionary Internship followed; this was a one year internship with modular classes while serving in an assigned church. After raising full support we were soon on our way to the Philippines by freighter, together with 5 other FEGC missionaries beginning their missionary careers.

Jack and Ella Sailor were in the workforce in Saskatchewan when they heard about ministry in Alaska.

It was late fall of 1970 or perhaps early in 1971 when our pastor, Rev. Homer Edwards, introduced a young man, Leander Rempel, a former student of his at Briercrest Bible Institute. He was now a missionary in Alaska and used the entire adult Sunday school hour describing the work of Far Eastern Gospel Crusade in Alaska.

He was, in fact, recruiting summer missionaries to help with building projects, on and off the headquarter complex in Glennallen. Children's ministries were held in many villages scattered throughout the state.

Jack and I looked at each other and smiled. We had always entertained the idea that we would go to Alaska one day. Up until this time they were recruiting only single young people, but since we had our own holiday trailer, Leander suggested we come for a few weeks. There would be plenty to keep us and our three children busy.

If Leander had plans for the rest of our lives, we never suspected. By the time summer 1971 was over, however, we realized that God Himself had a whole new role for us to fill. It was not to our liking. Absurd even! Whatever would He want with a police detective and a legal assistant/notary? We were imagining things.

Three stressful months later brought us to a powerful encounter with the Almighty. Revival had broken out in Saskatchewan. Night after night we were subjected to joyful testimonies of those who had met the Lord, then messages delivered by the Italian twins, Lou and Ralph Sutera. But it was on Sunday morning in Faith Baptist, our home church, when Rev. Carlin Weinhauer's message broke through our stubbornness. He unwittingly had drawn a picture of our lives.

We laid it all on the altar.

By 1976 we had completed studies at Briercrest Bible Institute and been accepted by Far Eastern Gospel Crusade for ministry in Dawson City in the Yukon. Our financial support was all in.

Warren and Dorothy Janzen served in Japan and now are in the International Office of SEND International.

How do you choose a mission organization? How do you make a decision which might impact the next 35 or 40 years of your life?

It was 1984, and the Urbana mission conference was coming up. The Lord very clearly was guiding me to a church planting ministry in Japan. Now I needed to choose an organization. Heading down to Illinois with three friends from Providence College, I made a plan to visit and evaluate all the organizations who worked in Japan.

Winding my way through the myriad of displays and the many invitations of helpful reps, I collected information on many good organizations who were working among the Japanese. I was looking for a match with my *calling*, to start churches among those Japanese who were beyond the reach of any local church. I was looking for an organizational *character* which valued teamwork, was willing to provide ongoing training, and which had fun together. I was looking for an organization which demonstrated some *competence*, whose members had a track record of actually accomplishing what they had set out to do. What I didn't realize I was looking for, but which played a big role in choosing SEND over the many other good organizations out there, was *chemistry*.

I had a number of conversations with mission organization reps, but one in particular stood out. That one where the guy wasn't simply interested in information. He wasn't just helping me understand and see the possibilities. That one conversation where it was obvious that the person I was talking to was sincerely interested in God's work in me—whether that would be with SEND or with someone else. The biggest demonstration of that happened when at the end of what I expected to be our normal conversation, the man asked if we could get away to a quiet place and pray together. His prayer was for God and me, not me and SEND. It was about the Holy Spirit speaking and guiding and providing. It was about God's agenda, God's timing, God's work in me.

Oddly enough, at a conference where hundreds of students are seeking the will of God for their lives, this man was the only person who asked to pray with me. A shock when I reflected on it later. Yet it was this time of prayer which set that person and the organization apart from all the other good organizations represented there. The man was Leander Rempel, then Canadian director for SEND International.

What I felt there was a bond of chemistry. It was reinforced through SEND Canada's diligent follow-up after the Urbana conference. It was reconfirmed when Leander came and visited me on campus later. There was a chemistry with this organization which helped me decide to make my commitment to missions in Japan through SEND.

Thus began a long journey with SEND. During my senior year at college the LORD brought Dorothy into my life. She had just completed two years as a nurse in Nepal and was committed to the unreached. We were married in August and were accepted by the Canadian council in December that same year.

Twenty-seven years later we've worked on two church planting teams, guided the Japan field as Area Director, and now serve as International Director and Women's Ministry

Team Leader. Twenty-seven years later the chemistry with SEND remains. An organization which is pursuing God's glory among the unreached, and God's leading in the lives of individuals. It was a prayer by one man in the bleachers of a university gym in Illinois that helped me decide to which mission organization I would commit. That prayer has led to a long obedience in one direction—to the unreached through SEND.

Dale and Teresa Murray sensed God leading them into ministry with SEND as they neared the end of their employment. They share:

God knows where we live!

It was our dream to retire early from our day jobs with enough youth and health to be significantly involved in Kingdom work.

After several years of praying and plodding, we came to an expectant resolve and prayed, "OK Lord, you know where we live, call us!"

Call us He did! Out of the blue one evening in January 1997 we received a telephone call. Leander Rempel, director of SEND International of Canada, introduced himself. He asked if we would consider the donor relations manager position. Before joining the mission we needed to raise our own salary—personal support!

We interpreted this as a God call and knew we had to investigate. Leander flew from London, Ontario to Swift

Current, Saskatchewan where we were living to talk with us. We questioned him over an entire weekend. We sensed the Lord's leading us to seriously consider the opportunity. We sought confirmation by speaking with our aging parents, those who would be left with responsibilities as they aged, and our church leadership, all of whom gave tremendous affirmation. Dale left 33 years of experience in executive management and Teresa her position as office supervisor with Canadian Automobile Association.

June 18th, 1998 we moved from Swift Current to London in a U-Haul truck. The Lord had provided the total financial support requirements, and the required number of prayer partners!

We soon discovered that Leander and then Martyn Hartley had cultivated and established relationships with donors from across the country. There were many faithful committed folks giving conservative amounts of monies monthly. One such person was always the first to respond to an appeal for funding for a special project.

SEND Canada was very much involved in helping to fund the construction of Kiev Theological Seminary in Kiev, Ukraine. God's provision was so apparent at one fundraising event in British Columbia. A couple first heard of SEND when their friend, a retired missionary, invited them to the dinner. Her description of the organization was that SEND was "very reputable." I'm sure she did not know she was being used of the Lord. The couple had a big tithe waiting for a big project and KTS became the benefactor that evening!

The Lord worked through us every day during our 12 years in the Canadian office under the directorship of Leander and later Rob (Mags) Magwood until our retirement in 2010. We were just ordinary people with an extraordinary God privileged in a small way to be making Christ known to a lost world by *mobilizing God's people* to *engage the unreached* in order to *establish reproducing churches.*[9]

14

Preparation and Orientation for Ministry

*T*he home staff was involved in preparing new missionaries for their overseas assignment. Upon arriving overseas, one of the first assignments for most missionaries was to learn the local language. SEND considered this to be of vital importance, since the missionary needed to effectively communicate to the local people. The Gospel speaks to the heart and that is best done in the language in which the people most naturally speak and express themselves. Along with learning the language comes learning the culture; the two are intertwined. Fluency in the language and adjustment to another culture take years of perseverance and intentional commitment.

Clive and Sharlane Donaldson were appointed by the Canadian board of directors to ministry in Alaska.

Following the candidate interview, it was on to Farmington for Pre-Field Orientation.

Then came deputation. Three months stretched to ten, but finally, at the beginning of June 1980, the long dusty road to Glennallen was driven and a new life began for the Donaldsons.

They arrived on a Saturday, and Rempels invited the Donaldsons and their Alcan traveling companions for Sunday dinner. In June, what else but fresh Copper River salmon would be on the menu? And Louise, in her gentle way, began "New Missionary Orientation" by explaining that, yes, even for a salad that is serving 14, there is only one tomato! To this day, Sharlane thinks of that first lesson in rural Alaskan grocery prices when she makes a green salad.

Terry Tiessen shares his experience:

I think my greatest ongoing challenge was the complication of ministering cross-culturally. In our first year, while in language school, we read *Growing Up in a Filipino Barrio*, and it taught us a great deal about how Filipinos think and feel, and how this affects their lives. I concluded then that I had come to the Philippines 25 years too late. I knew that I would never be able to think like a Filipino, or to act instinctively in a way that communicated my intentions to the people among whom we lived and worked.

Those were the years in which "contextualization" came into vogue, and much of what I read was helpful, but it also increased my sense of the difficulty of teaching theology in a contextually appropriate way. I was greatly helped by an article written by an American missionary (Dale Brunner) in the *South East Asian Journal of Theology*. He titled it (as I recall): "Singing the Lord's Song in a Foreign Land: Can a Foreigner Teach Theology?" I found very helpful his conclusions about the benefits of someone teaching from a foreign perspective, provided they are aware of that fact, and provided their students know how best to learn from their foreign teacher, including the need to ask themselves how they would deal with the Biblical material differently, from a cultural perspective, in their own ministry. For a number of years after reading that article, I shared the substance of that article with my students, in the first class of each of my courses. It did not diminish the difficulty of what I was doing, but it gave me peace and some confidence that I could actually bring to this task some helpful things which my Filipino colleagues did not, precisely because they were immersed in the same culture as their students.

SEND Canada has worked with both the US office and the International office of SEND to seek to provide effective orientation and preparation for each missionary. This has included church internships, language learning techniques, and cross cultural experiences, all intended to equip the individuals not only to adjust to another culture and language but to thrive in that culture and ministry.

15

Ministry

Once a level of language proficiency has been attained, the missionary has the joy of building friendships with the local people. They can begin to share Jesus with greater liberty and then disciple new believers, who will in turn share the Gospel with others and disciple them. Missionaries have the privilege of seeing believers grow in their relationship with the Lord and take more and more responsibility in the local church.

Ken and Bertha Guenther had this privilege when they were involved in church ministry in Baliwag, north of Manila.

One of the highlights that I have experienced a few times in my missionary career has been to see those whom I have trained or discipled or coached go on to lead in ways that far surpass what I could have done. Pastor Delfin Angad is one example. I discipled him when he first came to Baliwag Bible Christian Fellowship, and invited him to join our Kaagapay (like a small group) group that Bertha and I were leading. He eventually ended up leading our small Kaagapay group, and then becoming the pastor of the church after we left Baliwag. He then became the head of the Evangelism and Missions Department at ABCCOP, and now is the senior pastor of the Lipa ABCCOP church.

Pastor Derick Parfan, current pastor of Baliwag Bible Christian Church, is not someone I personally discipled or trained, but Bertha discipled his mother, and his father apparently came to Christ after one of my messages on Christmas morning! Derick is an amazingly gifted preacher even in English. He is leading the church into evangelism and missions in a way that I never could when I was the pastor/church planter in Baliwag. During summer 2013, he and 6 others from the Baliwag church went to Cambodia on their first international summer missions trip—with SEND! God has laid Cambodia on Derick and his wife's heart, and I will be very interested to see what God will do in the church and in the Parfans' lives in regards to this burden and vision.

Jack and Ella Sailor rejoice in lasting fruit from their ministry in Dawson City.

A special highlight for the entire body of believers was the baptism of eight adults in the slightly-above-freezing, but very beautiful, Ethel Lake. Four were new believers, the others having accepted Christ previously. Tears, laughter, hugs, and praises greeted each one as they came from the icy waters, and were swathed with towels and blankets.

Joyfully we can thank the Lord for the ongoing ministries of each one.

One couple studied at Briercrest Bible College. The Lord has blessed them both as a pastor couple and as church planters for more than 20 years. Early in their ministry they, together with their children, spent a year as missionaries in Papua New Guinea. The wife is a gifted author and speaker.

An RCMP officer came to know the Lord a year after arriving in Dawson. Shortly thereafter, he led his buddy to the Lord. His wife was a new believer. They were transferred to Prince Edward Island the week after their baptism and we enjoyed hearing of their growth in the Lord. Now retired, they still serve in their church, where he is an elder.

Another couple who had been involved in contracting and gold mining moved to Salmon Arm, BC, where they started a business. It wasn't long before he was elected mayor, and re-elected for several terms. Eventually he was persuaded to run for the federal election and has been re-elected a number of times. Watching their growth in Christ over the years has been a joyful experience. Their three children know the Lord; one of them is a missionary in Africa, together with her husband and children.

One of the single men still lives in Dawson City and serves the church and community in many ways. He is always busily involved in children's camp, tending the church building, and teaching and preaching when needed. We have enjoyed interacting with him as he continues to study the Word and to follow the Lord.

The other single man did not remain so for very long. A carpenter by trade, he moved to Vancouver Island where he met his life mate. They have busied themselves in sharing the Lord as He brings opportunities. They have a grown son.

Through the years of ministry God has taught us that He is faithful. He never gives up though inwardly at times we might lose hope. He showed us that He is our protector in a collision on winter highways; when our car stalled at –40 in the night; when spinning out of control on an icy hill and hanging over a cliff.

God was our provider. God led us to those in whose heart He had created a hunger for Himself. God led us to study, teach and preach His Word to those he had prepared. During our 11 years, God brought hundreds of people to our door seeking shelter and sustenance. He sent them to us because He had previously blessed us with food from forest and stream (moose, caribou, salmon). We were never short of something to share with those who were desperate.

Terry and Gail Tiessen saw fruit through teaching in a college and then seminary setting, and in a home Bible study.

I learned early in my teaching ministry what a great privilege it is to have time to study God's Word and to pass on what I have learned to students, watching many of them go on to serve the Lord well in spheres much larger than the one God gave me. I think for instance of Efraim Tendero, whom I remember as a very gifted freshman student. Efraim later became our pastor at Kamuning Bible Christian Fellowship, and now serves very effectively as the national director of the Philippine Council of Evangelical Churches. Hundreds of other students, from many different denominations, and from other Asian countries went on to serve the Lord faithfully in various ways, and I consider it a great privilege to have had a small part in their ministry formation. It was particularly gratifying to see some of my highly gifted students at Asian Theological Seminary go on to doctoral work and then return to take their place beside me on the faculty. I had many opportunities to learn from them in that peer relationship, where they ministered easily within their own culture.

Two areas come to mind when I think of Gail's satisfaction in ministry in the Philippines. The first was the ladies' home Bible studies which she taught for many years in Manila. I was excited to hear of women who first came to faith in Jesus as their Saviour through her ministry in those Bible studies, and to see some of them engaged in ministry of their own in later years. In our last few years in the Philippines, I watched the ministry Gail had to younger women missionaries from various missions, as they sought her out for friendship and advice in their own missionary struggles.

Ted and Sally Baker, serving in SEND North, describe an incident that affected them powerfully about 13 years ago.

We visited a woman from Faro while she was in the hospital in Whitehorse. We weren't close friends. Her reputation in town was her unabashed vulgar language and pride about being "one of the boys." Not exactly the church-going type, nor remotely interested in spiritual things. This visit was only because we were visiting someone else that day and heard she was in too.

We held a polite conversation with her, nothing too probing or even spiritual for that matter. Her diagnosis was not good so we avoided digging into that part of her life. As we were ready to leave we asked if we could pray for her, something we always do when visiting in the hospital. We left feeling as if we did the pastoral, neighbourly thing, nothing more.

Rewind to another incident when, sitting on a school council meeting, the chairman sailed into me [Ted] with such anger and vitriolic language I had a hard time composing myself. The specifics are not significant, just that this moment severed any friendship we had and any future relationship we might pursue. We never talked again after that. He eventually got a job in Whitehorse, much to my delight I might add.

The lady in the hospital died from her illness not long after we visited. Being the "somebody" she was in town, her funeral service was held in the town recreation center to accommodate the large crowd. I had a small part in the service, reading some opening scripture, and sat facing the large crowd along with others who participated in the service. Following me was the school council colleague, a close friend of the deceased. His comments were so unexpected it took all I could do to sit still and look normal. Here's what he said:

"I saw E—— in the hospital just before she died. She was giddy with delight, I've rarely seen her so happy, and I had to ask what had her so upbeat. She said 'Ted and Sally came by to visit me'" (he turned to look at me as he said this) "'and they prayed with me.'"

My emotions ran the whole gamut. I was humbled beyond words to think that a simple, half-hearted prayer could be such a blessing. I was convicted to the core to think that my anemic effort was used by God. I was astonished to think that this fellow, with whom I had done battle, would reference this incident and all but give me a compliment, in front of the whole town no less. I was speechless as I was awash with God's graciousness, using me despite my obligatory—and little more—effort.

Why was the woman so moved? Was it because she knew of her reputation and didn't feel worthy of being prayed for? Was it because she knew a preacher would hardly ever give her the time of day, yet I did, if only for a few moments? I could speculate much more, and will never know the truth. All I need to know is, God can use our weakest, shallowest, less-than-honouring efforts and turn them into a glorifying moment in ways we can never imagine, and probably will never even know about.

Laverne Fehr served in the Philippines from 1976 to 2001 and then in the home office.

For many years young ladies had come from Cagayan, the northernmost province on the eastern side of the Philippines, to work for missionary families in Metro Manila. While working, they heard the Gospel and trusted Christ as their Lord and Saviour. As they grew in their faith, they were burdened for their families. Missionaries and Filipino pastors desired to begin a church plant but there were no available personnel. Finally in the late 1970s there were several new missionaries who arrived and were willing to serve in Cagayan.

Laverne Fehr was one of the first missionaries to move to Tuguegaro, Cagayan, and this was her main area of ministry until 1990. Laverne and other team members were privileged to see the church grow from almost nothing to a group of believers meeting in a church building with national leadership.

The Lord worked in the hearts of people as they began studying the Word of God. The first years the Bible studies were mainly evangelistic. One study was in the home of L.U. As she and others in her neighbourhood studied the Word, she came to a deep and personal trust in the Lord Jesus. Her husband also trusted the Lord as his Saviour. Both became active in the new church that was coming into being. L.U. was quiet but always ready to share the Gospel with someone.

One person with whom L.U. shared was the pharmacist in the pharmacy near her home. The pharmacist, M.L., was very active in her religious group; however, she also wanted to study the Bible. So, she first attended her afternoon religious meeting and then came late to the Sunday afternoon Bible study in Laverne's living room. The Bible study at that time was mainly to ground believers in the Word but anyone was welcome. The group studied books of the Bible almost verse by verse. There was good interaction. M.L. had many good questions; the Holy Spirit was working in her heart—tearing down false teaching and beliefs and replacing them with Truth. It wasn't long before she arrived on time; she no longer went to her afternoon meeting! And in time she personally trusted Christ and followed Him wholeheartedly.

There were many other men, women, youth, and children who came to know the Lord. One of the key means of establishing the young believers in their faith was discipleship.

Many were discipled individually or in small groups. As they grew in the Lord, they were encouraged to disciple others; this is when the truth of the Word is solidified in their lives.

We cannot ignore the importance and absolute necessity of sharing and teaching the Word of God. God takes His Word and gives understanding to those who are reading it for the first time and brings light and freedom as the Truth sets them free.

Sherri Ens has served in Macedonia since 1998.

God puts us in the right place at the right time.

My co-worker and I moved to the eastern edge of Skopje in 2001. In the neighborhood where we believed that God had led us to work, there were two ladies who were already believers. One of these ladies had a sister who lived near me in an apartment, and I used to visit her, spending time with her and sharing about Christ. This happened for close to a year. While she had some interest, she never made any real decision to follow Christ. She was planning to move out of the area, and the day before her move, I went to her apartment to help her with some things.

Earlier that same day a new family moved into the apartment above her. They had met and talked … how they got on the topic of God I don't know, but this family of four wanted to hear about God. When I arrived, we went upstairs to talk with them. The husband fired questions at me for hours. Finally (at midnight) I excused myself and said I had to go, but I promised I'd come back and visit again, and I invited the wife to our upcoming ladies' outreach.

He is now the main leader in our church plant; she helps with children's classes.

That first year they brought to the Lord two other complete families (relatives of theirs), and they were all baptized together the following summer. All three families continue to be a part of our church plant, following God. And how did I meet them? One day overlap in the apartment building of the sister of a friend. Had they come a day later, or had she moved a day earlier, we may never have met.

Only God can bring people together like that. And I had the privilege of being that first person to tell them about Christ's love—that's a gift God gave me.

Jon and Elaine Winter are serving in Japan where the seed of the Word may be sown many times before they see it sprout and grow. What joy when someone embraces the Truth!

Elaine and I are reaching out to Japanese people through a Family Life Group. We had the joy of seeing a lady come to know the Lord and then be baptized. That can be said in a short sentence but covers a much longer period of time that began before we ever met her.

Mrs. M got to know about God at the church kindergarten where she attended. Her teacher was the pastor's wife, and was a very gentle, warm person. She heard the story of the God of the Bible, and prayed in the kindergarten. She wished that there was a God in her mind.

Sometimes Mrs. M went to the church when she was an elementary and junior high school student. Because she moved and changed schools a few times, she stopped attending the church.

Mrs. M married, and her daughter was born. Her daughter entered an international preschool at the age of two years. A lot of love poured out from Christian teachers for her daughter. She was really happy every day. This brought back memories of being similarly wrapped in warm love when she was in kindergarten. Her heart burned with a desire to know God more and more.

When her daughter was in kindergarten, Mrs. M became acquainted with "N" and Elaine. She joined the Bible study. To that point in time she thought that if she believed in God, it was good enough. She also thought that God didn't need her.

She knew she was not a good person. She knew she had disobeyed God's teaching many times. As a result she thought herself useless to God. However, her daughter didn't doubt that God loved her very much. As she continued to attend the Bible study, she gradually came to learn that God loves everyone.

"For God so loved the world that he gave his one and only Son."

Mrs. M knew how deep God's love was, *but* hadn't realized how wide God's love was. Mrs. M had been given the opportunity to know God many times but she had not been able to hear what He was saying to her in His Word. Now she began to understand that God's love is so large that He is able to pour it into all people. While she had committed many sins in her life, she now understood that her biggest sin was not believing in the big love of God.

After she joined the life group, she began to think about God's plan for her. She began to think about baptism. Until then she had thought that to be baptized and become a Christian were distant goals in her life. When it was possible to become a good person, she thought that she would be able to become a Christian by being baptized for the first time. Mrs. M thought that it would be a long time until that would happen because she [believed that she] didn't yet qualify to be baptized. She hoped to hear God's word about the plan to prepare her for baptism. Then, God suddenly gave her one verse. *"Repent and be baptized, every one of you, in the name of Jesus Christ for the forgiveness of your sins"* (Acts 2:38).

When she saw the Bible verse in the life group, she was really surprised. She thought that I had chosen this verse because I knew the hesitation in her mind. This verse pierced and stuck with her. She noticed that it was a voice that God had given through me and the life group.

Is it now or is it a future plan?

Mrs. M hesitated and spoke to "N" about her feelings. "N" said that God prepares everything for now—for the present. Mrs. M decided to entrust God with everything.

Baptism was no longer a goal but a step of obedience.

Mrs. M's prayer was "I have decided to turn away from sin and live the way that You want me to live. I commit my life to You. Lord Jesus, I thank You for saving me. I thank You that my sins have been forgiven and You have given me a new life."

Laura Bonney was part of a team the Lord used to teach Biblically-based values in public schools.

Heaven will tell the full story of what God has and continues to do through the ministry of VOICE Philippines, which keeps expanding throughout the Philippine Islands, reaching over 200,000 students weekly. My co-worker Ruth and I have been privileged to sit in the front row and watch God work as He has opened the door for the proclamation of values from His Word in public school classrooms.

In 2003 Pastor Tony Elizaga urged us to consider training volunteers to teach Biblical values in the schools. Churches wanted to teach Biblical values but didn't know what to teach since there was no curriculum available. Through much prayer, working with our Filipino colleagues, and the support of SEND International, God birthed VOICE—Values Orientation In Classroom Education. VOICE has a vision to see elementary and high school students "rooted in Biblical values for personal and national transformation." The name is also a connection to the ministry of John the Baptist, Luke 3—a voice in the wilderness (of public schools) to prepare the way of the Lord.

Just as the initial curriculum was being finalized in 2004, newly re-elected Philippine President Arroyo directed the Department of Education to allow non-governmental organizations (NGOs) of various religions to help teach values. The door was wide open. By the end of that first year, six churches were involved, three elementary and four high schools, seventy-three classes, and about 4,500 students. Humbled and thrilled by the reports from excited volunteer teachers, additional modules were developed by a growing Filipino curriculum team who often raced to have the next set of lessons done in time.

It has been a thrill to see God birth VOICE Philippines and provide in unusual ways. The largest individual donor involved in this project has been a cross cultural missionary from another mission! A foundation gave three significant grants to enable production and publishing of the sixteen volumes, the final module being completed in April 2012.

Another great joy has been observing God give favor with the Department of Education. The Values Curriculum uses the Bible as the text book and includes stories of Bible characters, plus Filipino and other heroes who exhibited particular values in their lives. One verse per value was put to music and taught/sung as part of the weekly class. The final (twelfth) lesson of each module includes a Gospel presentation woven around the two values that module has focused on.

Has it made a difference? One principal has cited positive evaluations from students from the Values Classes and insists that there has been a 60% decline in problems brought to the guidance office due to the Values Instruction Class program in his school. Other examples of transformations have been documented—cell phones returned; a teacher's wallet found and returned; a sum of $90 found by three students and returned to the owner.

Of course, the greatest thrill is hearing of students and their families coming to Christ as their Savior, especially through the follow-up programs and home visitation, and then being baptized and actively participating in the churches who sponsored the values classes. We praise God for the privilege we have had of encouraging churches to be salt and light in their community, raising their voice for the Savior. All praise to Him.

Jake and Lillian Leyenaar served in the Philippines and then in the Canadian home office. In 2007 they returned to ministry in the Philippines.

The SEND Philippines office and guest house were based north of Manila in Karuhatan, Valenzuela from day one (1947). By the mid-80s, traffic congestion and frequently flooded roads in rainy season made travel to and from Karuhatan difficult and time-consuming. In the late 80s the decision was made to re-locate to Quezon City. Separate lots were found for the office and guest house.

Standard building procedure in the Philippines includes erecting a sturdy wall around the perimeter of the property. A solid concrete-block wall was built to protect the guest house property from intruders. As soon as that was done, it was used as a support for a temporary road construction shanty on the boulevard between the street and the wall. The shanty was made of several sheets of plywood fastened to 2 x 4's, and covered with assorted sheets of roofing, with some split bamboo beds inside for the construction workers. When the road project was completed, the construction shack was not dismantled or completely vacated. One of the workers decided it would be an economical solution to his family's housing needs.

The lack of sanitary facilities, the hazards of open fires for cooking, fighting cocks wandering and defecating in front of the guest house entrance, occasional drunken brawls and noisy radios all added up to a not-so-good neighbour situation for our manager and guests. Efforts were made to get the family to move. After all, it was against the law to make a dwelling in that space. Appeals to the municipal authorities were fruitless because the squatter had friends there, and his influence among the urban poor of the area represented votes. So it remained a rather tense and unsatisfactory stand-off, somewhat tarnishing the pleasure of having a new, conveniently located guest house.

In September 2008 Lillian and I moved to the "long term apartment" in the guest house building. It was directly over the wall from the squatter, with only a carport-width separating the 2 dwellings. By now, the shanty had been cemented, had water, sewer, and electric connections, was divided into 3 small rooms, and had a small sari-sari (variety) store inside, accessed through the only window. We recognized that the possibility of the squatter abandoning his dwelling and moving away was next to nil.

We made various attempts to greet Mang Juan*[10] and his common-law wife Nina* (his wife had died some years earlier), but were basically ignored, or very coolly acknowledged. Often buddies of Mang Juan came by to have a drink with him,

---

10 Names marked with * have been changed.

along with discussing the beauty or prowess of some of their fighting cocks. Alcohol was a problem for Mang Juan.

In May of 2009, Lillian and I left for an eleven-week home service in the US and Canada. We came back to Quezon City in early August, to find unknown occupants in Mang Juan's house. We soon learned that they were grown children of Mang Juan who moved in so no one else would occupy the potentially vacant house. They told us that their father had suffered a stroke in early June, and he was staying near the ocean to recover from his paralysis. Ocean air is deemed to have medicinal value.

Several months later, we learned that Mang Juan had returned. He couldn't stand or walk, and basically lay on a small cot in the dark recess of the entrance room. Soon after that I visited him on a Saturday afternoon, read some scripture and prayed with him. He couldn't say more than a few words, but his tears flowed freely. I did this for a number of weeks, and then also gave him a Tagalog New Testament. Even if he couldn't say much, I knew he appreciated the visits.

With extra activities, and travel in December, it was a while before I got back to him. When I did visit him again soon after Christmas, I asked him where his New Testament was. He told me that Nina had taken it with her when she had left him. Apparently there had been conflict between her and his grown children, and she had returned to her family. Mang Juan was further bruised by this loss, compounding his physical infirmity.

It was an April morning when I was going out to jog that I was very surprised to see Nina sweeping the sidewalk beside their house, and in front of our gate. I couldn't help but express surprise in seeing her. She seemed friendlier than before, and further surprised me by saying she had been born again! She then asked where she might find a church of a specific denomination. I told her I wasn't aware of one nearby, but I did know that about 100 metres around the corner there was a good Bible church. I went on with my jog, realizing I had more bounce than usual! When I got back, I was excited to tell Lillian about this development, and encouraged her to visit with Nina. Lillian confirmed with her that the nearby church was a good choice.

We then told them that we would accompany them to Diliman Bible Church (DBC) that Sunday. Mang Juan led the parade in his wheelchair with the rest of us strung out behind. Immediately after I stood to introduce the visitors, Mang Juan and Nina, I became aware of some rustling around me. Fred*, a member of the church, stood to thank us for bringing Mang Juan and Nina. It turns out Fred was a neighbour in the urban poor area and was burdened for Mang Juan. He owned and operated a tricycle (motorcycle with sidecar, used as a short haul taxi), and Mang Juan also owned several of these units.

From then on, Fred and several other drivers visited Mang Juan at his house. It wasn't long before he accepted the Lord as his Savior, and was later baptized. He faithfully attended the Sunday service at DBC and also started coming to the early Saturday morning Bible study I was conducting at our place for neighbourhood men. He was a happier and friendlier man, having also stopped his smoking and drinking. Mang Juan gradually recovered some speech, and with persevering help from Nina, learned to walk a bit as well.

He is now no longer a thorn in the flesh, but a new brother in the Lord!

16

Trials in Ministry

The Lord continues to mold and grow the missionary's relationship with Him as they serve.

Doug and Lynn Harder served in the Philippines and then in North Central Europe, living in Czech Republic.

How does one begin to describe the things our family went through during the month of April 2005?

On April 1st our daughter Quinea was finishing up a three-day trip to England with her good friend Rebecca and family at Land's End. Riverside School (in Prague) was on break and Rebecca's family was hosting the girls. On the journey to the Bristol airport for their return flight to Prague, Quinea's health began to rapidly deteriorate. At the last possible moment Rebecca's mom sensed God prompting her NOT to put Quinea on the flight home. Instead she called an ambulance at the airport and had Quinea whisked away to the hospital. Quinea was rushed to ICU where she was ventilated, sedated and treated for shock.

Lynn and I had just arrived in Rome for the weekend to celebrate our 20th wedding anniversary. While standing inside St.

Peter's Basilica we got the news on my mobile phone. Amazingly, we caught the last flight out of Rome for London, and then drove through the night to be with our sixteen-year-old daughter. We didn't know if she'd be alive or dead when we arrived, but found her clinging to life in critical condition with a severe bacterial infection. It would be thirteen days before doctors would identify it as staphylococcal aurea, which caused a rare syndrome known as toxic shock.

After responding positively to antibiotics, Quinea was moved from the ICU into a hospital ward. But even as Quinea began to recover physically, she began to spiral downwards into confusion, fear and paranoia. Lynn and I could not leave her side day or night.

During one of the darkest nights of the soul for me as I sat beside Quinea's bed, God directed me to read Genesis 22 to her. As I began to read the story, it dawned on me that the chapter wasn't so much about Isaac (though his life was on the line) as it was about Abraham. God was testing Abraham to see if he feared God to the point of giving up his dearly-loved son. In an instant I realized that the crisis was not so much about Quinea as it was a test for Lynn and me. Did we fear the Lord enough to offer up our daughter? We had built a lot of altars over the last five years in coming to the Czech Republic. But now the Lord was asking us to build another one. And so in the dim light of the hospital ward, I built another altar and offered up my precious daughter.

Through all the agony that Quinea experienced in those dark days, her faith shone through the cloud of confusion. She hung desperately on to the Scriptures I would read to her. Without notice she would break into songs of worship to Jesus, sometimes in English, and sometimes in Tagalog. When I reprimanded her for singing so loudly in the middle of the night, she would just sing all the louder. And the patients in the long row of beds beside her told me to just let her sing. They had never heard anything like it!

For almost two weeks Quinea did not sleep. Then after a seemingly endless series of tests and transfers from ward to ward, Quinea began to break through the physical trauma and psychological quagmire. Quinea was moved to the Children's Hospital and began to recover.

During those nights, watching over my daughter in her hospital room, I was reading a book by Sheldon Vanauaken called *A Severe Mercy*. One evening while Quinea and I talked and cried together, it struck me that the title of the book described exactly what we were experiencing. We had been struck down in a crisis most severe. But through the severity of our ordeal, God was showing us unparalleled mercy. God was accomplishing something far deeper than just the restoration of Quinea's physical and mental health. And it became crystal clear to us that God needed to break into our lives and take us far away from Prague to bring renewal to our whole family. God orchestrated these events to bring us to England where he would show us a severe mercy.

Quinea's stay in hospital in Bristol would last thirty-five days. The cost would be in the thousands of pounds, but the Bristol Royal Infirmary covered every penny because of an agreement the Czech Republic had signed with England only the year before. As Czech residents, we were fully covered. Moreover, all our personal expenses for flights and accommodations were covered almost exactly to the dollar by the generosity of gifts we received from others. We were in awe of God's provision.

On May 5th we returned home to Prague. Quinea was convinced she had been given a second chance; a new life. A few weeks later, Riverside School allowed Quinea and her friends to hold an evening of worship and testimony. Many high school students came out, representing diverse nationalities from all over the world. That night Quinea and the worship team almost blew the roof off with their songs of praise. We will never be the same!

/7

Career Missionaries and
Short-Term Teams

*T*he Lord has used short-term teams and individuals in a variety of ways to engage the unreached. These short-term workers spent anywhere from a few weeks to a year on assignment cross-culturally. Some home staff missionaries also took teams to the field on numerous occasions.

Since SEND's field strategy was team ministry, a short-term worker could be assigned to a team of resident missionaries. Serving with a number of missionaries gave more exposure to a variety of ministries as the short-term worker spent time serving with each team member. They lived, ate and slept with the onsite missionaries. There was accountability and supervision. Before departure from the field, the short-term worker was able to transfer new contacts to the resident missionaries.

Some missionaries said that they didn't have time to give care to missionary wannabes. However, if the short-term program is run well, it will attract candidates to the program and the missionary task. While providing short-term teams or individuals with profitable, effective opportunities for ministry was time- and cost-consuming, the short-term program did contribute to the advancement of the Gospel. Short-term workers have assisted missionaries already on the field through encouragement, meeting new people, and providing additional manpower for specific ministries. In addition, the impact on the church overseas and in Canada was profound.

The short-term program also aided the spiritual growth of the short-term worker. This began before the individual left for their cross-cultural assignment, as the home office staff provided orientation and assistance in preparing for the short-term ministry. These were seen as key aspects of the program; they were not optional. The orientation included how to communicate with supporting churches and individuals, what to expect cross-culturally, how to maintain one's spiritual walk, how to deal with culture shock, and other important issues. Mentoring and orientation continued on the field, since missionaries were sensitive to the adjustment and needs of the worker. By the same token, debrief on the field and after return to Canada enabled the short-term worker to process more fully the experience and solidify it in his or her life.

Martyn Hartley has taken many teams to minister to the Chinese diaspora. Martyn and team used the train as the venue for sharing the Gospel with Chinese people going from Russia to China.

It was March 2007 in the Moscow train station. Martyn Hartley and Chinese team members dashed through the snow to catch the night train going to Beijing. They would spend three days and twelve hours on the train before disembarking in Ulan Ude, Siberia where the train turned south to cross the border into Mongolia. The purpose of the trip was to share the Gospel with Chinese people who were returning to China. This trip had been planned and prayed over for a number of months and now was finally happening. The workers had a copy of the Jesus film to share with Chinese passengers. They also distributed tracts and spoke with as many people as possible. There were quite a few who accepted the Lord on that first trip, but the team decided that the timing was wrong—they needed to do this just before Chinese New Year.

The next year saw another team on the train again but this time it was just before Chinese New Year. To their disappointment there were only a few Chinese people—only those who hated to fly direct to Beijing took the train. There were many tourists and they were able to lead a young Frenchman and a young Russian to Christ. Virtually no converts! Why? What was wrong—why were they there? Sometimes on a trip to Russia the workers would see many come to Christ, other times only two or three. They were, therefore, accepting of God's sovereignty, yet still felt the need to ask "why?" On the team was a brother who had seen nobody come to Christ after nearly three days on the train. "What am I doing wrong?" he asked. "What are you saying?" Martyn asked in return. "I tell them if they don't become Christians they'll die and go to hell!" he replied. "Well that's OK … but why not tell them how God changed your life from being a dishonest man to a worker in the church?" He immediately left the car and went to lead two men to Christ.

Upon arriving in Ulan Ude there was ministry awaiting the team amongst the Chinese community. They went for supper at the home of a colleague, Gardner, who had invited two Chinese students who were open to the gospel. The team was able to lead them to Christ!

Then the team met with Brother Sun who lives there and gives leadership to the church. He explained that he'd been waiting for the team as there were about twenty students who had believed over the winter and wanted to be baptized. We had the joy of seeing these believers in Jesus baptized.

By the end of the evening Martyn's leg was swollen as a result of slipping on ice at the train. What a pitiful old man! "No worries," said the young brother from the team. He went to the restaurant and got a small glass of vodka, to which he set fire. He then proceeded to massage the hamstring with hot vodka. Now it did hurt! Gardner was on the phone with Martyn during the massage and heard the scream of anguish. He brought Tylenol for the flight home. The vodka worked because in the morning Martyn was walking without a problem. Praise the Lord!

The Canadian team members began their flight back to Canada while the Moscow team members travelled home by train. Once again the Moscow team had the privilege of leading others to Christ while riding the train.

Albert Wai has taken teams to East Asia and has seen God work in the lives of those to whom they ministered.

"My food," said Jesus, "is to do the will of him who sent me and to finish his work. Don't you have a saying, 'It's still four months until harvest'? I tell you, open your eyes and look at the fields! They are ripe for harvest" (John 4:34-35).

As a short-term English ministry team member, one could well be led subconsciously to see oneself simply as an English teacher, not as a minister. Summer 2008 was the typical example. Eleven of us set out for Macau for over a month of teaching small children and high school teens. The team was serving with the local church and the resident missionary, Eva Watt.

The team members arrived a few days in advance and by Friday, most things were in place to begin ministry the following Monday. Eva invited anyone in the team who so desired to go on a Bible and tract distribution stint on Saturday that was organized by other peer mission groups in Macau. Most of the team joined the evangelism effort.

Our team members were brought to probably the busiest tourist spot in Macau. They were each given packets of evangelistic materials and Bibles. Once a tourist bus stopped, a couple of our team members and other local believers would scatter around the bus, making sure everyone alighting from the bus would be given a set of those materials. That was it; they were not expected to engage the tourists in conversation.

After about 3 hours, they all came back, excited as ever!

"Daisy led two tourists to Christ right then and there near the buses!" they told me. Other team members were asking and talking with her about exactly how that happened as they stepped into our conference room coming back.

Daisy gave the books out; two of the tourists took them and asked what they were. One then somehow kept asking questions, listening to Daisy's answers, sharing her feelings, asking more questions, and then she was willing to accept Christ as her personal Saviour. The other one kept listening in. After seeing one conversion, she asked her own set of questions, listened to Daisy's answers, shared her feelings, and soon also accepted Christ as her personal Saviour!

The following day, Sunday, we went to Eva's church for service. As was the practice, we arrived a little early, trying to get more interaction time with the congregants.

Very soon, Eva took Daisy to sit with an elderly lady and they began talking. During the service, Eva informed the congregation that Mrs. Lee, sitting next to Daisy, had accepted Jesus Christ as her Saviour just before the start of the service. We praised the Lord for her repentance in Christ. Hallelujah! A few days later the church pastor, Eva and Albert went to her house to take down the idols in her house.

We praised the Lord for the three conversions in two days even *before* any of the team's teaching ministry began in Macau! By the end of the one-month teaching, out of about thirty high-schoolers, three recommitted themselves and six came to Christ, including the one big guy who was the chatter box of the class from the first day! Just incredible!

The most precious lesson was that as ministers of the Gospel, we always have to be consciously aware of all our surroundings and not only aware of the task we were specifically called to do in a set scenario.

We must take the ministry responsibility on as our skin, and not our clothing.

Changes in Ministry Assignments

*T*here are times when ministry assignments change while overseas. The opportunities are multitudinous and personnel are limited. Missionaries train national believers for the work of the ministry and then move on to other areas where the Gospel has not yet been heard. In some situations it is necessary for a missionary to assume a responsibility because there is no one else to do work that simply has to be done. One of the qualities of a good missionary is flexibility.

Clive Donaldson has experienced the need to learn new responsibilities during Clive and Sharlane's ministry in Alaska.

Leander's confidence that Clive's potential exceeded his current abilities once again expressed itself when, soon after his arrival, Clive was asked to computerize the mission. This was no small assignment, involving the offices and accounting records of three institutional ministries. This would have been easier if Clive had had a bookkeeping background and if his computer education had not been in programming block-long computers of the early 70s. But with an accounting course and the help of some Christian computer professionals, he was able to accomplish this task in fairly short order and keep everyone working with the benefits of automation for years to come. By the time he was asked to become the field treasurer, a decade later, he had learned that the tasks God assigns are accompanied by the wisdom and ability needed to fulfill them. A lesson learned from the example of Leander Rempel, whose own life and ministry exemplified it.

The Donaldsons speak in 2013 about God's faithfulness over the years. Although it is just one of his tasks, Clive has worked with missionaries regarding their financial support. Perhaps not ironically, this has been one of the biggest challenges for the Donaldsons personally. Many times they have said that when the financial ability to remain with the mission ends, they would know it was time to quit. Supported through a variety of non-traditional means, they have nonetheless been able to continue in ministry with SEND, and with 40 years of service seemingly not too far down the road, it appears their career ministry will have been just that, a full career! It is clear that God has kept them in Alaska all these years. Through good and bad times for the mission, good and bad times for them, He's been working to build His Kingdom in the North. What better way to have spent their lives?

While the SEND Canada office was in the process of relocating to the London area, the Lord was working in the heart of Eva Watt. She was very involved in recruiting and working with applicants but she also was sensing the call to return to Hong Kong to a church ministry. The Lord confirmed His leading and her home church commissioned her in 1992 to this new ministry.

The Lord has given fruit in the church in Hong Kong and since 2005 in Macau.

Doug and Val Clutton served in the Philippines from May 1988 to January 2002.

The latest craze among the boys of Ligao is collecting a cannibalistic variety of spider and pitting them against each other to see whose will come out the winner. In order to find these spiders, one has to look carefully among the grasses, trees and bushes to find a "silk." Upon finding one, it is lightly plucked to tempt the spider from its hiding spot thereby enabling the crafty boys to catch it and put it into their "kulungan" (match box).

Aside from the rather gruesome illustration, this fad got me thinking about spider webs and how they relate to our lives (I married a Webb, so I ended up with lots of Webbs related to me!). God has already planned before we were born what we are to do for Him. I feel as though we must seek the various strands of *our* web and give them a little pluck once in a while to know which is ours, and which does not relate to His will for us. This can be a very complicated, sometimes confusing search, but with prayer, and an eagerness to search for God's will in our lives, I am convinced that He will not lead us astray. He will also give a lasting peace about our direction.

Over the past years, we have had to pluck numerous "silks" and often been rewarded for our persistence and diligence. Looking back over my life, I can see how God has clearly woven a beautiful web in which I have found challenge, growth, fulfillment and peace. First I see that God clearly led me into audiology and even looked after the details of Bible training in between. He then went on to lead me clearly to the Philippine field with SEND International as the channel of His grace. There have been many difficulties, hardships and even discouragements, but I have never regretted the path. I believe we are and have been where God intended us to be. I believe He has used this web to shape and mature our lives to conform to Him.

As we began to pluck the various silk threads that came our way over the past couple of years, we have come closer to seeing a clear direction. At first, I gave up audiology entirely, never really expecting to use those skills in any significant ministry. But there always remained the nagging question: "*why* all the training?" and the nudge not to let go of my credentials. Then in the ministry here in Ligao, we have seen how God has given us fruitful spiritual ministry among the deaf through various venues but also seen fit to give us not just a small, but a large and ever-increasing professional platform for ministry.

With FCHC (Fishermen of Christ Hearing Center) now widely recognized by the government in this region (now working towards a second accessible venue for a clinic), we have seen the potential for ministering not only to the deaf who are known, but identifying increasing numbers of spiritually deaf so that they too can "hear" the good news. We distribute tracts to those who come for evaluation, and we have a growing network of doctors and government officials who recognize and appreciate the professional quality of our services—thus lending great credibility to FCHC. These too are ties to building relationships that could lead to salvation.

When Martyn and Jill Hartley were serving in the Donor Relations department of SEND Canada, he was challenged at a church meeting in Toronto to work with a particular need in China. To his surprise, Jill readily agreed to go, and Leander gave them his blessing for the ministry. At the end of their time in China the Lord opened another door to ministry with Chinese people through a burden placed on Leander's heart.

On a trip in Khabarovsk, Russia, Leander was struck by the number of Chinese businessmen on the train with huge bags of wares to be sold. He saw these people again at the kilometer-long row of kiosks in the market area. Leander saw them as people who needed to hear the Gospel, and as far as he knew, there was no one who was reaching out to them. These Chinese people were in Russia for a short time and would soon return to their home country, so they needed to be reached during that small window of opportunity. Leander wondered who could go and struggle with all the challenges that would be there in this kind of ministry. Martyn came to mind, and when approached, he was willing to pick up the challenge and be an instrument in God's hands. Martyn is an entrepreneur missionary who has been tremendously used by the Lord in evangelism. He is very aware of his dependence on the Lord, and at the same time very aware of who his Lord is, and that He can and will do beyond what can be asked or imagined. Martyn has seen hundreds of people come to know the Lord Jesus as their Saviour, and has been involved in arranging training for these new believers.

Doug and Lynn Harder were in a fruitful church planting ministry in the Philippines. The Lord used them to establish a church and they completed the task. They then sensed God moving them on to the Czech Republic, since the Philippines had many healthy churches, while the Czech Republic was predominantly atheist, having many cities and towns with no gospel witness. This meant once again starting from the beginning in a new language and culture. They left a culture that was warm, open to the Gospel, and very responsive. They went to a new culture that was self-sufficient, had no basic belief in God, and was not readily responsive. They remained steadfast in their commitment to serve God where He had led them.

God has been and continues to be at work in the lives of Canadian men and women, and he uses many of them in various SEND ministries around the world. He is bringing each one to a place of abundance in their walk with Him and also bringing many thousands of people from other countries to a place of abundance in their relationship with the living God. This is His work and we are privileged to be involved in a small way in what He is doing.

The Book of Acts never really ends. Through the centuries the work of the Holy Spirit has gone on and on and on.

*B*etween the covers of this book we have endeavored to tell you how God moved in powerful and mysterious ways to bring SEND International to Canada. However, it would have been a tragedy if SEND had just hunkered down and praised God for the privilege of bearing the secret things of God to other countries. God intended that Canadians rally to the cause and spread the gospel worldwide, including our own country.

We ask ourselves, "What is this 'Gospel'?" Paul made it very clear in his letter to the church that met in Rome. In Romans 3:23a he says, *"for all have sinned and fall short of the glory of God."* He repeats that in Romans 6:23, *"For the wages of sin is death."*

While mankind had no way of finding God, God was reaching down to mankind. *"But God demonstrates his own love for us in this: While we were still sinners, Christ died for us"* (Rom. 5:8). *"But the gift of God is eternal life in Christ Jesus our Lord"* (Rom. 6:23b).

This eternal life is a free gift, but it must be received in order for us to complete the transaction and in order for it to be of any value to us personally. The only way this can happen is if we exercise faith in Jesus Christ as the payment for our sin.

"Therefore, since we have been justified through faith, we have peace with God through our Lord Jesus Christ" (Rom. 5:1). We are no longer separated from God, but now have peace with Him and He lives within us through the Holy Spirit.

Paul sums it up this way: *"If you confess with your mouth, 'Jesus is Lord,' and believe in your heart that God raised him from the dead, you will be saved. For it is with your heart that you believe and are justified, and it is with your mouth that you confess and are saved"* (Rom. 10:9-10). *"Therefore, there is now no condemnation for those who are in Christ Jesus"* (Rom. 8:1).

If you have never received this Gift, we would invite you to accept it now.

If you have received this Gift, we invite you to join those who are sharing this Gospel around the world.

Afterword
By Rob "Mags" Magwood

In 2004 I had the honour and challenge of stepping into Leander Rempel's shoes. While I appreciated his nomination and unwavering support, I have called him many times since to ask *"What in the world have you gotten me into?"* We laugh together, and marvel at what God has done (and continues to do!) through SEND Canada. I still look forward to our calls.

At the time of our transition, Leander had given primary leadership to SEND Canada for more than twenty years. He and Louise seemed to know everything about SEND, missions in Canada, and everyone involved along the way! Their gracious mentorship has been a great help and blessing, for which my wife, Kathleen, and I thank God.

Isn't it wonderful to read stories of God's faithfulness? This written record of lives changed by the Gospel illustrates the diverse ministry the Lord is accomplishing through SEND, along with many related challenges and blessings. I'm grateful for Leander's work, and Laverne's able assistance, in assembling this account of our first forty years—now others will benefit from this story of God's goodness.

Since its inception in 1963, SEND Canada's leadership has shared the vision that SEND must continue to be a learning organization. This means the unending pursuit of preserving our essential core while seeking to bring about healthy change.

Some things about SEND Canada, then, have not changed. We remain firmly committed to the Word of God and our core values, including the urgency of proclaiming the Gospel due to the lostness of humanity, and making disciples of all the nations. We also hold that the church is the primary stakeholder in the Great Commission, and that SEND is a servant agency.

But some things about SEND are changing! Through God's goodness, we have "worked ourselves out of a job" in some areas where the work of expatriate personnel is completed, and are now redeploying to new people groups. Emerging strategies of Tentmaking and Business as Mission (BAM) are enabling us to engage yet unreached people. New technology and the migration of people groups into diaspora are changing how and where we do our work. And in one of the most exciting developments, new mission personnel are increasingly joining SEND from other parts of the world. The growth of our new offices in Asia and Latin America reveals that God is continuing His work!

So the first forty years of SEND Canada chronicled in these pages form both a legacy *and* a foundation. Evidently God's work in this hurting world is not yet finished, and we earnestly desire that SEND Canada continues to be a useful tool in the Lord's hands. As in the early days, we depend upon God, and seek to serve with courage, creativity and a collaborative spirit.

Let us watch, pray, and work hard until that Great Day when our King comes again!

Rob "Mags" Magwood,
Director of SEND Canada
April 2014

Appendix A
Career Missionaries

Allen, Gordon & Lisa
Andrews, Jim & Ruth
Au, Peter & Mable
Austring, Brent & Lynn
Baker, Ted & Sally
Barg Thiessen, Jonathan
& Corrie
Barkman, LeRoy & Marcella
Bonney, Laura
Brubacher, Dave & Martina
Burkhart, Rachel
Bush, Ken & Marie
Callaway, Dan & Lynn
Cavenagh, Patrick & Marianne
Chen, Rita
Chui, Jo-Jimmy & Maylin
Clutton, Doug & Val
Crichton, Heather
Davis, Janet
Donaldson, Clive & Sharlane
Donovan, Fiona
Ens, Sherri

Essery, Ione
Fast, Elvin & Della
Fehr, Laverne
Fehr, Leigh & Jana
Ficzere, Heather (Quiring)
Flower, Carol (Poley)
Frentz, Steve & Jennifer
Geddert, Len & Marrian
Geldart, Andrew & Bev
Gogel, Merla
Guenther, Ken & Bertha
Hamm, Renata
Harder, Doug & Lynn
Harms, Dennis & Sally
Hartley, Martyn & Jill
Hartshorn, Laurence & Debbie
Janzen, Warren & Dorothy
Jovellanos, Darlene
(Armstrong)
Koning, Steve
Kuka, Sam & Melody
Lam, Katharine

Lam, Tom

Lau, Daniel & Gretel

Lawrence, Audrey

Leschied, James & Molly

Leshuk, Carter & Christine

Leyenaar, Jake & Lillian

Liu, Stephen & Nightingale

MacCullum, Muriel

Macfarlane, Sharon

Magwood, Rob & Kathleen

Mahaffey, John & Andrea

Martinez, Amy (Hochachka)

McKay, Bruce

McLaughlin, Bob & Trudy

Miles, Cathleen (Ten Brinke)

Murray, Dale & Teresa

Nalos, Richard & Jackie

Olney, Phil & Claudia

Omelchuk, Val

Oshiro, Roy

Paetkau, John & Leanne

Penner, Ken & Myrna

Peters, Dorothy

Peters, Milt & Kathy

Price, Winifred (deceased)

Reimer, Margaretha (deceased)

Rempel, Barry & Ruth

Rempel, Leander & Louise

Rieger, George & Kathy

Rollings, Trent

Sailor, Jack & Ella

Sapelak, Adam & Angela

Schultz, Dave & Barb

Seib, Rod & Eileen

Stobbe, Miriam

Tanaka, Miwako

Tazumi, John & Edith

Tazumi, Tom (and Mary, deceased)

Thiessen, Larry & Joyce

Thiessen, Ray & Lisa

Tiessen, Terry & Gail

Tucker, Sue

Vencio, Ed & Marlu

Wai, Albert & Daisy

Watt, Eva

Wicker, John & Sharon

Wilton, Greg & Patti

Winter, Jon & Elaine

Wong, Wilson & Teresa

Yung, Circle

Part-time Office Employees

Cleland, Elizabeth

Gibbison, Elaine

Koning, Dave

Lightbody, Stuart

Appendix B
Board of Directors

August 1965 — Phil Armstrong (President); Virgil Newbrander (Vice President); Arnold Barkman

December 1965 — Phil Armstrong (President); Virgil Newbrander (Vice President); Arnold Barkman (Secretary Treasurer); George Loewen (guest)

August 1966 — Phil Armstrong (President); Virgil Newbrander (Vice President); George Loewen (nominated as member); Harold Fife (nominated as member)

August 5, 1967 — Phil Armstrong (President); Virgil Newbrander (Vice President); George Loewen; Harold Fife
    Nominated Stimers, Clymer, Crump, Miller, Fife, Hendrix, Loewen to Canadian Council that was to meet on August 14, 1967 in Toronto area. Appointed Stimers as chairman pro tem.

Gordon Stimers: August 1967 – November 2013; 46 years

Ronald Miller: August 1967 – November 1977; 10 years

Arthur Clymer: August 1967 – August 1985; 18 years

William Crump:	August 1967 – November 1980; 13 years
George Loewen:	August 1965 – September 1989; 24 years
Harold Fife:	August 1965 – 1976 (listed as Ex-officio in July 1976; listed with Corporation Members as of June 30, 1978; not on list for 1979-80)
Sid Kerr:	September 1969 – June 1978; 9 years
Ken Hanna:	February 1975 – November 1982; 7 years
Gordon Dorey:	September 1969 – September 1986; 17 years
John Klassen:	June 1976 – March 1997; 21 years
Jim Vold:	June 1978 – March 1984; 6 years
Stan Karram:	May 1983 – August 1993; 10 years
Byron Hand:	November 1996 – June 1998; 2 years
Art Schmidt:	August 1992 – September 2002; 10 years
Claude Pratt:	May 1991 – November 1995; November 1998 – September 2004; 10 years total
Fred Tiessen:	February 1983 – October 1991; 8 years
Terry Tiessen:	September 1986 – March 2001; 15 years
Jean Barsness:	December 1983 – present
Richard Quiring:	December 1983 – present
Ted Cossitt:	March 1999 – present
Rod Masterson:	November 2002 – present
Harold Barg:	June 2003 – present
Charles Cook:	November 2005 – present
Doug Harder:	November 2008 – November 2013; 5 years

Appendix C
A Brief History of SEND Canada

1945   US ministry formed under the name of Far Eastern Gospel Crusade (FEGC) by American GIs affiliated with the GI Gospel Hour during WWII. Missionary focus on Japan and the Philippines

1963   Far Eastern Gospel Crusade of Canada incorporated in Manitoba

1966   First Board of Directors meeting in Toronto

1975   Dr. Russell Honeywell assumes responsibilities as first full-time Canadian Director

1976   First office dedicated exclusively to the work of FEGC Canada

1981   Bill Wallace appointed interim Canadian Director

1981   Leander Rempel appointed Canadian Director, moving to Toronto area in 1983

1982   Far Eastern Gospel Crusade of Canada becomes SEND International of Canada

1992   Canadian office moved from Toronto to Komoka, Ontario, west of London

1993   Fire destroyed the entire complex containing the Canadian office

2004   Rob Magwood appointed as Canadian Director

Bibliography

Givens, Elizabeth M. and Reapsome, James W., editors. 1984. *With my Heart There: Excerpts from the writings of Philip E. Armstrong*. Farmington, Michigan: SEND International.

Givens, Elizabeth, editor. 2007. *Footprints…Values of a man who walked with God*. Farmington, Michigan: SEND International.

Morehouse, Mildred M. 2001. *Through Open Doors: A History of SEND International*. Farmington, Michigan: SEND International.

SEND Canada Board minutes

SEND Canada files

SEND Canada Member Manual

Alliance of Bible Christian Communities of the Philippines, "History." Accessed April 3, 2014, at http://www.abccop.org/history.html.

"History of the Japan Evangelical Missionary Association." Accessed April 3, 2014, at http://www.jema.org/joomla15/index.php/who-we-are-topmenu-27/15-history-of-the-japan-evangelical-missionary-association.

"Records of SEND International – Collection 406." Accessed April 3, 2014, at http://www2.wheaton.edu/bgc/archives/GUIDES/406.htm.

If you would like to know more about this ministry, contact
SEND International of Canada in the following ways:

Website: www.send.org/canada

Telephone: 1-888-918-5036

Email: info@sendcanada.org

About the Authors

Dr. Leander Rempel graduated from Briercrest Bible College and the University of Detroit, and later received an honorary doctorate from Briercrest Theological Seminary. As a visionary, a man of prayer and faith, and a skilled counsellor, Leander is a servant leader and has been used by God in both the pastorate and mission leadership. He and his wife Louise have three married children, who are all involved in active Christian ministries. The Lord has blessed the Rempels with seven grandchildren.

Laverne Fehr is a graduate of Millar College of the Bible and Briercrest Bible College. She was accepted by SEND Canada in 1976 and served in church planting and administration in the Philippines. Since her return to Canada, she has performed administrative roles in the Canadian home office.